BAPTISM

CONSIDERED IN RELATION TO ITS MODE & SUBJECTS

GREAT CHRISTIAN BOOKS
LINDENHURST, NEW YORK

BAPTISM

CONSIDERED IN RELATION TO ITS MODE & SUBJECTS

ARCHIBALD
BURGESS

Great Christian Books
is an imprint of Rotolo Media
160 37th Street Lindenhurst, New York 11757
(631) 956-0998

Burgess, Archibald, 1790 – 1850
Baptism / by Archibald Burgess
p. cm.
A "A Great Christian Book" book
GREAT CHRISTIAN BOOKS an imprint of Rotolo Media
ISBN 978-1-61010-024-3
Recommended Dewey Decimal Classifications: 200, 202, 230, 265
Suggested Subject Headings:
1. Religion—Christianity & Christian theology—Baptism
2. Christianity—Bible—Sacraments, other rites & acts
I. Title

Book and cover design are by Michael Rotolo, www.michaelrotolo.com. This book is typeset in the Minion typeface by Adobe Inc. and is quality-manufactured on acid-free paper stock. To discuss the publication of your Christian manuscript or out-of-print book, please contact us.

Manufactured in the United States of America

CONTENTS

PREFACE

To those who have long looked for the appearance of these sermons in print, it will be a sufficient excuse for the delay of their appearance, when I remind them of the repeated and long-continued afflictions of my family by sickness, so that I have not, till recently, been able to attend to the subject.

These discourses were originally prepared by the author, for his own congregation, without the remotest idea of their publication. And it was after much hesitation, and with the advice of some of my brethren in the ministry, that I consented to their publication.

The author designed to exhibit a very plain scriptural and historical view of the subjects upon which they treat, designed for plain readers. Some things are repeatedly mentioned, and designedly so, that they may not be forgotten.

They are now given to the public, in the hope that they may enlighten some minds, scatter doubts which have been created in others, and establish those into whose hands they may fall, in the truths and promises of the everlasting covenant of God, that "the blessing of Abraham may come upon them." If they shall, to a greater or less extent, have this effect, the purpose of their publication will be answered.

THE MODE OF BAPTISM
—PART ONE—

DISCOURSES I AND II

"Go ye therefore and teach all nations, baptizing them in the name of the Father, and of the Son, and of the Holy Ghost." —*Matthew 28:19*

This command of the Lord Jesus Christ was given to his disciples, in his last instructions after his resurrection, and prior to his ascension. In these words, his disciples were commissioned, and required to teach or disciple all nations—or to preach the gospel to every creature. In these words was also instituted originally Christian baptism, as an ordinance of the Christian religion, during the latter dispensation. And the form of baptism is here so clearly specified, that it cannot be mistaken. I have selected this text for the purpose of bringing before my hearers the subject of Christian baptism—concerning which, there has been, and still is, much unhappy controversy among the disciples of the Prince of peace; controversy that is prejudicial to the

interests of true religion; destructive of the spirit of piety
and godliness; of brotherly kindness, Christian fellowship
and communion. The subject of the mode of baptism is
frequently so introduced, and pressed upon the consideration of the anxious and yet impenitent inquirer after
the way of life, as to turn away the mind from the great
work of the soul's salvation, and fix it upon the mode of
performing an outward ordinance. Instead of "What must
I do to be saved?" the mode of baptism then becomes the
all-absorbing question, and powerful revivals of religion are
stalled suddenly in their progress.

There are times when duty imperiously demands the
consideration and discussion of Christian baptism, both
as to its mode and subjects. Such a time, my hearers, as
it seems to me, has now arrived. I have not now brought
forward this subject, because there is any peculiar pleasure
in discussing controverted doctrines; but because it has
been thrust upon the public mind, and because it is
important that we should have f correct views upon all
subjects connected with the religion of Jesus Christ; that
we should not undervalue the subject under consideration,
nor yet attach an importance to the mode of administering
an outward ordinance, which is not attached to it in the
Scriptures, and which, therefore, does not belong to it. It is
manifest from the text, that baptism itself is an important
institution, required by the express command of the great
Head of the church, the King in Zion. This is universally
admitted. There is "One faith, One Lord, One baptism."
Baptism is now the token of God's covenant, and the
"seal of the righteousness of faith." It is also a symbolical
washing, or purification with water, representing the
inward purification of the heart by the baptism of the
Holy Ghost, when God pours out his Spirit, or rains down

righteousness, like showers that water the earth.

In baptism, water is to be applied to the subject in the name of the Father, and of the Son, and of the Holy Ghost.— And this is to be done by one ordained to the work of the ministry of reconciliation. Concerning the form of baptism, and the fact, that the administrator should be one ordained to the work of the gospel ministry, there is no question; all are agreed; there will, therefore, be no occasion to discuss those points at this time; but I proceed to consider,

I. *The Mode of Christian Baptism*

For about three hundred years past, it has been contended, by some, that the mode in which baptism is administered, is essential to the validity of the ordinance. Others suppose, that all that is required to the validity of baptism is, that water be applied to the subject in the name of the Father, and of the Son, and of the Holy Ghost, and by a duly authorized person. By the former class a supreme importance is attached to the mode in which the ordinance is administered, as it regards visible membership in the church of Christ; and by such, probably nine-tenths of all the church are put beyond the pale of the visible kingdom of Christ, because they have not been baptized in a mode which they think essential.

It is admitted, that if either Christ or his apostles have any where prescribed the mode in which baptism is to be administered, then all ought to practise that mode: but if no such mode is prescribed, then we have the right, in common with others, of judging concerning the mode; and none have the right to utter a sentence of excommunication, because we cannot see with their eyes, nor understand in accordance with what we believe to be their errors.

Upon this subject, no one is asked to believe this or that way to be right, merely because I assert it to be so. Assertions prove nothing. And yet this is a subject, concerning which much bold and confident assertion is made. Things are boldly asserted, which never have been, and never can be proved. I do not, therefore, expect to establish my views by assertions; for when a thing is merely asserted, and as promptly denied, both sides stand precisely upon the same ground, till the proof is offered upon one side or the other. The subject before us is the mode of administering baptism. It is a controverted subject; yet we (that is, those who hold to the views of the speaker) do not wish it to be understood that we have any fears from the discussion of it, or that we keep the subject of baptism out of sight in regard to those who are candidates for our church fellowship. We consider our views of the subject as abundantly sustained, both by the testimony of the Scriptures, and that of history.

The more I contemplate and study this subject, the more thoroughly am I confirmed in the correctness of Paedobaptist views. It is important that we have a clear understanding of the subject under consideration. It is not whether sprinkling, or affusion, or immersion, is baptism. Some affirm that immersion is absolutely necessary to the validity of Christian baptism: consequently they reject, as pertaining to the visible church, all who have not been immersed; and therefore refuse to commune with them in the ordinance of the Lord's supper, as members of the household of faith.

I shall attempt to show that the Scriptures no where prescribe immersion as the mode in which, only, baptism can be administered, and that sprinkling, or affusion, when administered by an authorized person, and in the prescribed form, is valid baptism.

It is passing strange, that if Christ had intended that immersion should be the only good and valid baptism, that he should not, in some of his instructions, so clearly and definitely have described the mode, that no sincere inquirer after truth should fail of discovering it. And it is stranger still, that many, after they have, in their own estimation, discovered where immersion is thus prescribed, should afterwards entirely lose sight of it, and be led, as they have been, to doubt whether it be in the Bible, and finally to become satisfied, that there is no such mode prescribed. But still, I make it no proof upon this subject, that many have renounced the exclusive views of the Baptists, and joined themselves to the Paedobaptists, as did a minister and almost his whole church in Rhode Island, not long since, and several ministers with whom I have been personally acquainted. On the other hand, Paedobaptists frequently adopt the exclusive views of immersionists.

In discussing this subject, I shall necessarily have occasion to speak of those who differ from me; yet I trust, that it will not be in the spirit of unkindness, but in the spirit of love and in defence of the truth.

And although it is said by our opponents that we follow the traditions of men; and that the reason why we are not with them is, that we are unwilling to take up our cross and follow Christ; yet I will not return railing for railing,—and only say, that we have carefully, and with prayer, sought after the truth, that we might know what the Lord will have us to do: and yet we have not been able to find any instructions in the Scriptures, prescribing immersion as the mode in which, only, baptism can be rightfully administered; nor any precept, either in the letter or spirit, by which we are authorized to exclude from the church those who entertain views differing from ours in relation to the mode of baptism. In other words, we do not consider the mode in which a person has been baptized, essential to a regular standing in the Christian church.

We admit that immersion is baptism: but we object to the inference, that because this is one way in which baptism may be administered, therefore it cannot be lawfully administered in any other mode.

We admit that Christ has prescribed "one baptism" as to form, with water, in the name of the Father, and of the Son, and of the Holy Ghost; but has no where prescribed the mode; this he has left to the judgment of men, their sense of propriety, decency, and convenience.

Having premised these remarks, I proceed to the examination of the subject. Is then, immersion essential to the validity of baptism? That immersion is baptism, I have already admitted; and I have no disposition to deny that immersion has been more extensively practised in some ages of the church than it is at present; but that it was ever universally practised, or that it was practised at all by the apostles, or in their days, has never yet been proved.

It is said that the word *baptizo* always means to immerse, to bury in water. If this be so, then the question concerning the mode of baptism is forever settled, and all persons professing the Christian religion ought to be immersed. It has been a thousand times asserted that *baptizo* means to immerse, and never any thing else; but this does not prove it. I have thought that the more ignorant some are as to the meaning of the word, the more confidently the assertion is made, that *baptizo* means invariably to immerse.

It is said that if the translators of the Bible had rendered the word *baptizo* by immerse, there had been no question about the meaning—but then they must at the same time have destroyed all Greek literature, or it certainly would have been discovered, that they had not given the only meaning of the word.

In answer to the above assertion, we may say that, if the translators had uniformly rendered *baptizo*, to sprinkle; and *baptisma* and *baptismos*, sprinkling or affusion; then there had been no question as to their meaning, and baptism by sprinkling or effusion, had been the universal practice. But still it would not have stood the test of examination. When it is asserted that *baptizo* means only to immerse, it is a sufficient answer to this assertion to deny it; and the denial is as good as the assertion, till the assertion is proved; but it never has been proved: yet it has been so often and so confidently asserted, that many have thought that the assertion must be true.

I shall undertake to show that this word cannot always mean to immerse; and that it has not necessarily that meaning in any case in which it is used in the New Testament.

1. The word is used in cases where water is applied only to a small part of the body.

Mark says, chapter vii. verses 2-4, And when they saw some of his disciples eat bread with defiled (that is to say, with unwashen [aniptois]) hands, they found fault. For the Pharisees and all the Jews, except they wash [nipsontai] their hands oft, eat not, holding the tradition of the elders. And when they come from the market, except they wash [*baptisontai*[1]] they eat not. Matthew also says, xv. 2—Why do thy disciples transgress the tradition of the elders? for they wash not [niptontai] their hands when they eat bread.

Here the part of the body to which water was applied, was the hands. But *baptizo* is said to mean always and only the putting the whole body under water: but in the cases above mentioned, the hands only were wet, and they constitute but a small part of the body. Mark uses the words nipto and *baptizo* as synonymous. Nipto never signifies to immerse, but to wash by the application of water; and yet he uses *baptizo* in the same sense, to wash the hands by the application of water; sometimes by taking up water with the hands, and sometimes by having it poured on them by another person.

Again, it is said, When they come from the market, except they wash [*baptisontai*], are baptized, they eat not. In this case the word *baptizo* is used where it cannot signify the immersion of the whole body; but evidently the washing of the hands.

Luke writes thus, (chap. xi. 38,) "And when the Pharisee saw it, he marvelled that he had not first washed, [ebaptisthe]," had not first been baptized, or baptized himself before dinner; that is, had not regarded the tradition of the elders, and washed his hands before he ate. It will never be made to appear with the shadow of probability, that all the Jews immersed the whole body every time they came from the market, and every time they ate; yet on these occasions they were uniformly baptized. This baptism was simply a ceremonial purification from uncleanness, supposed to have been contracted by being in company with, and touching those persons or things that were ceremonially unclean. The above is another instance of the use of the word *baptizo*, in which it does not signify the immersion of the whole body, but the application of water to the hands only.

2. The word *baptizo*, and its derivatives *baptisma* and *baptismos*, are used in relation to the application of water, when the things to which the water was applied could not conveniently be immersed.

In Mark vii. 4, it is said, "And many other things there be which they have received to hold, as the washing [baptismous, baptisms] of cups, pots, brazen vessels and tables." This was the universal practice among the Jews in all their families, received by tradition from the elders, and this was daily practiced. Some things may have been immersed when they were washed; but to say nothing of the other articles mentioned, who can for a moment suppose that all the tables in Judea were daily immersed, some of them large enough to accommodate large companies? I am aware that some in this place, instead of tables, read couches; that is, the couches on which they reclined at their meals; but this will not help the idea of immersion in the case; and this washing, in whatever manner done, was a ceremonial cleansing; and if the couches received this cleansing, it may very rationally be supposed that a Jew would sprinkle them. But if we understand tables as in our translation, (and according to Schleusner's Lexicon the translation is correct,) then it must be supposed that they were washed, or received their baptism by the application of water. Then, if some were washed (baptized) by being immersed, and others by the application of water to them, it is manifest that *baptizo* does not always signify to immerse, nor its substantives always immersion.

3. The word *baptismos* (baptism) is used in the New Testament, in which the writer himself defines it as including in its meaning sprinkling.

Paul in his Epistle to the Hebrews, chap, ix, 10, referring the Jews to their former services at the temple, says, "Which stood only in meats and drinks, and divers washings, [diaphorois baptismois, divers baptisms,] and carnal ordinances, imposed upon them until the time of reformation." Now what were these divers baptisms to which Paul refers the Jews? Something evidently with which they were familiar. And who is there that has ever read the account of those services of the Jewish church, to which Paul here refers, and calls baptisms, that does not know that the greater part of them—the most important, the most solemn and sacred part of them, were done neither by immersion, nor pouring, but by sprinkling? Who, that does not know that the baptism of the mercy seat—the baptisms of tents, vessels, and persons, by which they were to be purified for the service of the Lord, were by sprinkling—of blood, of the ashes of an heifer, and water? But that there might be no doubt that the apostle intended to include in his divers baptisms, sprinkling, he says, verses 13, 19, 21, 22, "For if the blood of bulls and of goats, and the ashes of a heifer sprinkling the unclean, sanctifieth to the purifying of the flesh."—"For when Moses had spoken every precept to all the people according to the law, he took the blood of calves and of goats, with water, and scarlet wool, and hyssop, and sprinkled both the book and all the people."—"Moreover he sprinkled likewise with blood both the tabernacle, and all the vessels of the ministry, And almost all things are by the law purged with blood." And this purging, or purifying, was by sprinkling; and these sprinklings the apostle Paul terms baptisms. The apostle Paul, then, did not understand the word *baptizo* to mean always to immerse, and its derived substantive *baptismos*, always immersion and nothing else.

4. It may be remarked that when the New Testament writers have wished to express the idea of immersion, rendered in English, to dip, to plunge, they have in no case used the word *baptizo*, but another word; and in the greater number of cases a compound, as in Luke xvi. 24; Matthew xxvi. 23; Mark xiv. 20; John xiii. 26; Revelation xix. 13. In these cases they use the root of *baptizo*, viz. *bapto*, prefixing perhaps a preposition. And this word *bapto* does not uniformly signify to dip, being otherwise used in the Scriptures; and in one of the above cases, that of the rich man, in his conversation with Abraham, in which he prays that Lazarus might "dip the tip of his finger in water," all that is necessarily implied is that he might wet "the tip of his finger" with water, and cool his parched tongue.

5. The apostle Paul in alluding to Christian baptism uses a word which does not ever necessarily mean immersion.

Writing to the Ephesians, and speaking of the church, he says, "That he might sanctify it and cleanse it by the washing (loutro) of water by the word." This "washing of water," refers to baptism, as baptism is the only rite in which water is used by the church. And when we remember what the apostle has written in his Epistle to the Hebrews, that he there defines "baptisms" as including the various sprinklings practiced in the religious ordinances of the Jews, we understand why he uses a word in relation to the ordinance of Christian baptism, both here, and in his Epistle to Titus, (iii. 5.) which does not necessarily ever mean immersion. And we may also understand why both Luke and Mark use the word *baptizo* in reference to a washing, in which only the hands were wet; because, *baptizo* does not always signify to immerse, for it signifies according to the use of these writers, both sprinkling and affusion, and it signifies to immerse only by necessity, that is, when such are the circumstances that it must be so understood.

I will only add here, that the seventy who translated the Old Testament into Greek long before the coming of Christ, in the passage in Daniel v. 21, which speaks of Nebuchadnezzar, and which, in our translation, is rendered "his body was wet with the dew of heaven," use the word ebaphe to express the idea; that is, the body of this king was baptized, certainly not by immersion, but by being wet with the dews of heaven. Now it is contended as one reason why *baptizo* ought always to be rendered to immerse, because it is derived from *bapto*, which it is contended means always to immerse or plunge; and that the derivative *baptizo*, means the same as the root *bapto*. But the above is an instance in which *bapto* is used with a meaning quite remote from any thing like to immerse, to be wet with the dew—and this, in the judgment of the seventy, was to be baptized with the dew. Now if *bapto*, the root, does not always mean to immerse, then much less its derivative *baptizo*. An instance in which *baptizo* is used in the Old Testament in which it cannot signify to immerse, is found in Isaiah xxi. 4. And if it is desired by any to know more about those "divers baptisms" mentioned by Paul, Leviticus xiv. may be consulted, in which he will find them to have been chiefly sprinklings.

It is clearly manifest from the foregoing, that by the New Testament writers, the words *baptizo*, *baptisma*, and *baptismos*, are not used in reference to immersion exclusively. The writers evidently did not understand them to mean, either literally or figuratively, in all cases, the plunging of the whole body under water. *Baptizo* is used in cases where no such meaning could possibly be attached to it. This being true, the whole argument derived from the meaning of this word falls to the ground. And the assertion so often made, that *baptizo* means only and always, the entire plunging of the whole body under water, cannot be true.

Before I proceed to the consideration of the cases of Christian baptism by the apostles, mentioned in the New Testament, I have a few things to say concerning the baptism of John. By those who hold to immersion exclusively, much stress is laid upon his baptism, especially in the case of Jesus Christ. The example of Christ! the example of Christ! in regard to baptism, is continually cried. And it is called Christian baptism, as though Christ was baptized merely for an example to his disciples. And it is taken for granted that he was immersed, and that for the purpose of showing his disciples how they must be baptized. Whatever might have been the mode in which John baptized, it cannot possibly be understood to be Christian baptism, for the following reasons—

1. John was born, performed all his works, and died, under the Jewish dispensation. He did not know even the form of Christian baptism; nor is there anything on record by which it appears that he had the remotest idea that such a thing would ever be introduced into the church.

2. John was the son of a Jewish priest, and consequently of the order of the Jewish priesthood—and his baptism was Jewish; he simply baptized his disciples with water, as a symbol of their professed purity when they confessed their sins.

3. Jesus Christ himself was born under the Jewish dispensation, and was circumcised and performed all his

"mighty works" under that dispensation, even to the bowing of his head upon the cross, and giving up the ghost. Then it was that that dispensation closed; the vail of the temple was rent in two, showing that the way to God was no longer through the Jewish high priest, but the way "into the holiest" was now opened "by the blood of Jesus, a new and living way, which he hath consecrated for us, through the vail, that is to say, his flesh." What therefore Christ Jesus did, as it regarded rites and ceremonies, which belonged to that dispensation, can never be an example for us; else we should be bound to practice circumcision, and keep the passover. In these things we have the example of Christ.

4. When Christian baptism was instituted, John had been dead for a year and a half. Baptism, as a Christian ordinance, was not instituted till after the death and resurrection of Christ—nor till the moment of its institution, is there the least evidence that any of the disciples had the remotest thought that baptism, as a perpetual rite, in the introduction of members to the Christian church, would ever be introduced; nor till years after it was introduced, that circumcision was to be done away.

5. It is a constituent part of Christian baptism, that the form prescribed by Christ be observed; viz. that it be administered in the name of the Father, and of the Son, and of the Holy Ghost. It is necessary to the validity of baptism, or indeed, to constitute Christian baptism at all, that it be in the form prescribed by Christ—"In the name of the Father, and of the Son, and of the Holy Ghost." It will not be pretended that baptism was ever administered in this form till after the ascension of Christ.

6. Christ was baptized not for an example to his followers, but to fulfil some existing law. He said to John, "Suffer it to be so now; for thus it becometh us to fulfill all righteousness." And what could be the meaning of this language, when used by the great High Priest, applying for baptism to a priest under the Jewish law? What was it that satisfied John that he ought to baptize Him, of whom he said, "He shall baptize you with the Holy Ghost and with fire." There can be no other meaning to the phrase, "fulfill all righteousness," but to render perfect obedience to an existing law, when the law under which the individual is acting is a perfect rule of duty. And if there be no precept in the law, either moral or ceremonial, to which this rite, in this case, was obedience, then may we admit it purely as an example. Now the law for those that entered upon the priest's office was, 'that they should be brought to the door of the tabernacle, and be washed with water and anointed with oil; and that, when they were thirty years of age. And this washing is designated as having been of the hands and the feet, to signify their moral purity when they went in to minister before the Lord;—see Ex. xxx. 19—21. This washing of the hands and the feet was repeated as oft as they went in to minister before the Lord. They were set apart to the priest's office, by washing with water at the door of the tabernacle, and anointing with oil. As to the mode in which this was done, we learn from Numb. viii. 6, 7. "The Lord spake unto Moses, saying, Take the Levites from among the children of Israel, and cleanse them. And thus shalt thou do unto them, to cleanse them: Sprinkle water of purifying upon them, and let them shave all their flesh, and let them wash their clothes, and so make themselves clean." So Christ Jesus, being of the legal age, that

is, thirty years old, and now about to enter upon the public ministry of the priesthood, rendered obedience to the above ceremonial law, and went to John, a priest of the order of Aaron, to be washed, or baptized—and he was immediately after anointed with the Holy Ghost sent down from above. He was not baptized to signify his pardon, or the removing of sin from his heart or life; for he was perfectly holy. Christ never did any thing merely for an example, and especially in regard to an ordinance which was not yet instituted. Whatever he did, arose out of the relations he sustained to God and the world, as the man Christ Jesus, and the mediator between God and man, subjecting himself to the whole law of God, both moral and ritual; and doing whatever became necessary to him to constitute him the accepted sacrifice for sin and the Redeemer of men. Christ instituted the ordinance of the supper, but did not partake of it—and just as he was about to ascend to heaven, he instituted the ordinance of baptism—so that had not Christ when he was now about to leave this world instituted Christian baptism, no one would have thought of following the "example of Christ" in baptism, any more than they would in celebrating the passover.

Much reliance is placed upon the baptism of Christ, as to the mode of the ordinance; and if this be the example which we must follow, we ought to be absolutely certain that we have the exact mode in which he was baptized, before we affirm that nothing else is baptism, and proceed to cut off from Christian communion and church fellowship those acknowledged to be Christians, only because they have not been baptized as we have. And is there any thing which makes it undeniably certain as to the mode in which Christ was baptized? The use of the word *baptizo* does not point out the mode, because, it has already been shown that it means washing, as when the hands are washed—that it includes in its meanings, sprinkling, as used by Paul to the Hebrews. Then, the mode in which Christ was baptized, must be learned, if ascertained at all, from the circumstances; and none of these are mentioned except by Matthew and Mark, who say, "he went up straightway out of the water." Admitting that he walked into the water, how was he baptized when there? There is not a word said about it. One takes it for granted that he was baptized by sprinkling, another, by pouring, and a third takes it for granted that it was by immersion; but Matthew says not a word about it, nor does Mark. Again. Every body that ever read the Greek Testament, knows that there is not any certainty that he stepped a foot into the water. It is well known, that apo, rendered "out of," is, in the greater multitude of instances in which it is used in the New Testament, rendered "from; "and this passage rendered accordingly, would read, "he went up straightway from the water."

It is said that John baptized "in the river Jordan;" so it is said he baptized "in Bethabara beyond Jordan," and that he baptized "in the wilderness." Putting them all together, do they mean, can they mean any thing more, than to specify the places where John baptized. Again, it is said, that he baptized "in Enon near to Salim, because there was much water there." Great multitudes resorted to John, and it was necessary that he should be in places where there was plenty of water for the use both of the men and their beasts. It is no evidence that he baptized by immersion—and travellers say, that Enon is a place of many springs—"polla udata" many waters—and in the whole history of John's baptizing, there is not, from any of the circumstances mentioned, any certainty that he ever baptized a single individual by immersion.

And then his baptism was not Christian baptism, unless Christian baptism was practiced long before the rite was instituted.

I next proceed to examine those cases, in which Christian baptism is mentioned in the New Testament. There are, I believe, only nine cases of baptism mentioned, without giving in any case a description of the manner in which it was administered. Had the apostles deemed the mode in which this ordinance is to be administered essential to its validity, and had they attached so much importance to it as is attached to it at the present day, by those who practice immersion exclusively, they would, undoubtedly, have been more frequent in their communications concerning baptism itself, and more definite in their descriptions of the mode. But they have only mentioned this subject incidentally, never stopping to describe the mode, nor to speak of the great humility of the disciples who were willing to take up such a cross as that of being immersed.

In the history of these cases there is not one word said, that goes to show that the apostles understood that it was essential to Christian baptism that it be administered in a particular mode.

Another fact we shall find in the examination of these cases of baptism, which is, that there is not in any one of them the remotest allusion to any movement from the place where they were, for the purpose of baptism, when they acknowledged their obligations to be baptized—wherever they were, there they were baptized, whether on the banks of a river, in the midst of a great city, in a prison, or in a private house.

When Christ Jesus was about to leave this world, he gave to his disciples the commission contained in the text, which commission included the instituting of the ordinance of Christian baptism. They received and understood it. They understood it as Jews, who had been accustomed to the purifications performed in the temple, the greater part of which were performed by sprinkling; and always by sprinkling when men were to be purified, with but very few exceptions. Christ gave his disciples no instructions how they should administer baptism, as to the mode. All that is essential to the validity of the ordinance he specified. When God deems any thing to be done by man essential, he tells him what it is, in language so clear and full, that it cannot be mistaken by the sincere inquirer after the truth. And when he deems the manner, or mode, in which a thing is to be done, essential to the right doing of that thing, then he points out that manner or mode as clearly as the thing itself, saying,—" See that thou make all things according to the pattern showed to thee in the mount; "so that all who desire to do the will of God, may do the things required, and do them in such manner, or mode, as shall be in accordance with the divine direction. These truths must have been perceived by all who have read in the Bible the record of God's communications to man. He gave a particular description of all the items that were to compose the tabernacle, and afterward did the same concerning the temple. Proceeding upon this principle, had God deemed the mode essential to the validity, or right administration of baptism, he would as clearly have pointed out that mode as the ordinance itself.

The first instance of Christian baptism after its institution, was on the day of Pentecost, when "about three thousand souls" were baptized. "Then they that gladly received his word, were baptized; and the same day there were added unto them about three thousand souls." Not a word is said how they were baptized—not a word about their moving from the place where they were. They received the word and were baptized. Not a word is said about their going "down into the water,"—of being "buried by baptism;"—nothing about "following Christ down to the watery grave," and the like; all that is said is— "they... were baptized." Attention to the circumstances will show a strong probability that they were not baptized by immersion; and indeed, that it was impracticable that they should have been.

On the morning of that day, the apostles experienced the fulfilment of the promise of the Saviour, that they should "be endued with power from on high;" afterward, they went out and began to preach the gospel to the Jews gathered at Jerusalem, from the surrounding nations, to celebrate one of their annual festivals; and in consequence of the miracle of tongues wrought that morning, they were enabled to speak unto them in the various tongues in which they were born. This was the third hour of the day, or nine o'clock in the morning. After this, time sufficient elapsed for Peter to preach his sermon, an abstract of which is given; then came the subject of inquiry, made by a great multitude, what they should do to be saved—when Peter preached to them again; "and with many other words" besides those written, "did he testify and exhort, saying, Save yourselves from this untoward generation." After this, on giving evidence that they had become the disciples of Jesus Christ, they were received to the church on that same day, by baptism.

Suppose now that the apostles immersed these three thousand disciples, and each of the twelve could have immersed one in two minutes, it would have taken them eight hours and twenty minutes; and if they could have done it twice as fast, four hours and ten minutes; but taking into account all the other transactions of this day, there evidently could not remain even the shorter period for this work. Besides, what man ever had physical powers sufficient to stand more than four hours in the water, and immerse one a minute; even granting that it may be done with this rapidity for a short time? And who at this day would be willing to undertake such a work, especially if he had to cut a hole through the ice, and the thermometer was from ten to twenty degrees below zero?

But some of those who hold to immersion exclusively, attempt to get over this difficulty, by saying that all the one hundred and twenty baptized. The one hundred and twenty included the women, and it is probable that the majority were women; and they certainly had not been commissioned to baptize. Others lug in the seventy, whom Christ once sent out into all the cities, whither he himself would come, to aid the apostles; but there is no evidence that they were ever commissioned to baptize. The supposition is without foundation, but necessary to help the Baptist out of his dilemma. There is not evi dence that even one of them was, at this time, in Jerusalem. The greater part of Christ's followers were, evidently, at this time, away in Galilee, from eighty to a hundred miles from Jerusalem.

Now is there any thing in this relation that favors the idea that these three thousand were immersed? Was it possible that they should have been in Jerusalem? There was no river there, no pond, and indeed no other body of water sufficient for this purpose, to which they could have had access. And the enmity of the Jews would scarcely have permitted' them the use of the public pools. And besides, there is no mention of their moving from the place where they were; nothing said about their going "down into the water;" of "following

Christ down to the watery grave;" of the astonishing sight of three thousand, in one day, buried in water, after the example of Christ. It seems to have been a great oversight in the historian not to have mentioned, and dwelt upon these facts. How natural, had this been the fact, that he should have done it, and then it would have settled forever the question of the mode of administering the ordinance of baptism. Instead of this, all he says about it is, that they were baptized. And is there any thing in this account of baptism, to which sprinkling or pouring will not answer equally well as immersion?

The next instance of baptism recorded, is that of the Samaritans in Acts viii. In this case, there are no circumstances mentioned, by which any thing can be determined concerning the mode. The historian does not tell us how the ordinance was administered,—he simply states the fact, that "they were baptized, both men and women."

The next case that occurs is that of the eunuch, baptized by Philip. Philip was directed to go and join himself to the chariot of the eunuch. He heard him read the prophet Esaias—from which he preached to him Jesus the Saviour. The eunuch believed, and requested Christian baptism. He said to Philip, "See, here is water; what doth hinder me to be baptized?" And the chariot, at the command of the eunuch, stood still, "and they went down both into the water, both Philip and the eunuch; and he baptized him. And when they were come up out of the water, the Spirit of the Lord caught away Philip." In this case, all the circumstances which were ever supposed to favor the idea of immersion, are expressed in the words, "they went down both into the water, both Philip and the eunuch;" and "were come up out of the water." To a mind little accustomed to think for itself, it may be made to appear quite plausible; nay, quite certain, that this was a case of immersion; for it says expressly, "went down into the water,... come up out of the water." Why go down into the water, if not for the purpose of immersion? Many have believed, and many a preacher has said, that going down into the water in this case, was going all over into the water—and that coming up out of the water, was a coming up from a literal burial in the water. But let us examine the subject, and see if these things are certainly so, or necessarily so at all. Going down into the water can mean, at most, only stepping into the water: and after they had stepped into the water, Philip baptized the eunuch. How did he baptize him? Going down into the water does not mean immersion, for then Philip must have been immersed as well as the eunuch. Philip went down into the water equally with the eunuch—and if this means immersion in case of the eunuch, equally does it mean immersion in the case of Philip. Did the eunuch go down into the water, and come up out of the water; so did Philip go down into the water, and come up out of the water. And if this phraseology necessarily implies that the eunuch was immersed, not less does it imply that Philip was immersed. And not only so, but as Dr. Dwight justly remarks, "Philip was immersed as well as the eunuch, and not only once, but twice, and the eunuch three times;" for after they had both gone down into the water, that is, were immersed, Philip baptized the eunuch, that is, as the Baptist says, immersed him. After this, they both came up out of the water, that is, after Philip had baptized the eunuch, they were both again immersed; so that Philip was immersed twice, and the eunuch three times—if going down into the water, and coming up out of the water, in this case necessarily implies immersion. And the administrator, as well as the subject, was immersed. But this will not be admitted. Then going down into the water, and coming up out of the water, does not mean immersion. Then, as before remarked, this phraseology can imply, at most, only that they stepped into the water: but how Philip baptized the eunuch is not said, nor is it even implied. Baptists say it was by immersion; but as the historian who records the transaction says nothing about it, and they do not tell us where they got this information, we must suppose they say it on their own authority. Travellers assert that there is not, on the route the eunuch was travelling, water sufficient for the purpose of immersion: also the account itself styles the region desert. Moreover, it seems manifest that the quantity of water was small, from the manner in which the eunuch called the attention of Philip to it—a little rill, or the like, that might not have been observed, unless attention had been called to it. He says—See, here is water. And after all, the language used in describing this transaction, does not necessarily imply that either Philip or the eunuch wet even a foot in that water. This, every one that can read the account in the original, certainly knows; for the prepositions here used, and rendered "into" and "out of," may with equal truth be rendered "to" and "from;" and this is the more frequent rendering of these words in the New Testament.

All then, that is implied in the narration of the historian is, that they went down, that is, from the chariot to the water, and came up from the water; or that they both went together down to the water, and Philip having baptized the eunuch, they returned from the water. And it may here be remarked, that in all the cases of baptism mentioned as having been administered by the apostles, this is the only one, in the account of which there is any mention made of approaching, or going from, going into, or out of, any water for the purpose of baptism, or of any motion from the place where they were, and here only from the necessity of the case; as travelling in a chariot they must stop, go down to the water beside the highway for baptism, and return that the eunuch might resume his journey.

The next case of baptism mentioned in the history of the Acts of the Apostles, is that of Saul of Tarsus, chap. ix. 18. With the account of Saul's conversion, every one is familiar. "Saul arose from the earth; and when his eyes were opened, he saw no man: but they led him by the hand, and brought him into Damascus. And he was three days without sight, and neither did eat nor drink." Ananias, directed by the Lord, "entered into the house" where Saul was, "and putting his hands on him, said, Brother Saul, the Lord, even Jesus that appeared unto thee in the way as thou earnest, hath sent me, that thou mightest receive thy sight, and be filled with the Holy Ghost. And immediately there fell from his eyes as it had been scales; and he received sight forthwith, and arose, and was baptized.

And when he had received meat, he was strengthened." In this case, all the circumstances utterly forbid the idea of immersion. The place was a private room in which Saul was confined; the situation in which Ananias found him, blind, and evidently very weak from having fasted three days. And it was after his baptism that he was strengthened by receiving meat. Ananias found him sitting, or lying in his room—and as he was, he laid his hands on him, and immediately he received sight, and arose, and was baptized. Not the remotest intimation is given of moving from the place where Saul had lain, blind and fasting for three days.

Nor is there the shadow of probability that there were any conveniences for immersion in the room where he was. Had he been disposed, Saul was not able to have repaired to any place for immersion. Manifestly the vision in the way had very great influence upon the physical powers of Saul, so that he was blind, and in connection with his fasting, his strength was greatly prostrated. This is also manifest from the manner in which his weakness is alluded to, in the mention of the fact that he was strengthened by the reception of meat after his baptism. All the circumstances of the ease, the order and manner in which these circumstances are narrated, show most conclusively, that Saul must have been baptized, either by sprinkling or pouring.

The next case is that of Cornelius and those that were with him. Cornelius had been instructed in a vision to send for Peter,—and he had called together at his house his kinsmen and near friends. Peter went and preached unto them Jesus Christ, the way, the truth, and the life; now for the first time understanding the Scriptures, that the Gentiles should be made partakers of the gospel of the grace of God—the prophecy which says, "And he shall sprinkle many nations;" and that in Christ Jesus all the families of the earth shall be blessed: and as he preached, "the Holy Ghost fell on them." "On the Gentiles was poured out the gift of the Holy Ghost;" and they spake with tongues, and magnified God. "Then answered Peter, Can any man forbid water, that these should not be baptized, which have received the Holy Ghost as well as we? And he commanded them to be baptized in the name of the Lord." What is there in this account that looks like immersion? Is it in the declaration of Peter, saying, "Can any man forbid water, that these should not be baptized?" Evidently this does not mean whether any would object to the use of a pool, pond, or river, for the purpose of baptism. Peter himself was persuaded to go to these Gentiles only by a special vision from heaven,—and was afterward blamed by his Jewish brethren for going to them. "And they of the circumcision which believed, were astonished, as many as came with Peter, because that on the Gentiles also was poured out the gift of the Holy Ghost." The subject was now presented to them in a new light, against which their prejudices were strongly rooted. They had seen the Lord extending equal blessings to the Gentiles, as to the Jews,—and evidently the amount of Peter's inquiry is, Can any of you of the circumcision, refuse Christian baptism to these Gentile converts, and reception to the church, "which have received the Holy Ghost as well as we?" And no one could make any objection, and they were baptized as Peter required. But how were they baptized? Nothing is said about going down into the water, or of going to any water, or even of moving from the room where they were. And they certainly had made no calculation upon being baptized beforehand. All that is said, is, that they were required to be baptized in the name of the Lord; and baptism, as we have already shown, may be the application of water to a small portion of the human body, a sprinkling. And it seems plain to me, that these disciples were baptized either by affusion or sprinkling. It would have been nothing strange if Peter, with his Jewish prejudices, and strongly attached as he was to Jewish practices, and Jewish modes of doing things,—so much accustomed as he was to symbolical purifications by sprinkling, and especially, when Christ had said to him, "He that is washed needeth not save to wash his feet, but is clean every whit," should have baptized these disciples by sprinkling.

The next case is that of Lydia, Acts xvi. 15. Paul and Silas, in their journey, arrived at "Philippi, which is the chief city of that part of Macedonia." The historian says, "And we were in that city abiding certain days. And on the Sabbath we went out of the city by a river side, where prayer was wont to be made; and we sat down, and spake unto the women which resorted thither. And a certain woman named Lydia, a seller of purple, of the city of Thyatira, which worshipped God, heard us; whose heart the Lord opened, that she attended unto the things which were spoken of Paul. And she was baptized, and her household." In this account, there is no allusion made to immersion, as the mode in which they were baptized; nor are there any circumstances mentioned in which allusion is made to such mode. They were indeed by a river's side—but they did not go there for the purpose of baptism. Paul and Silas went there to preach the gospel of the grace of God unto certain women, who, it seems, were accustomed to resort thither for the purpose of prayer. There Lydia was converted, and baptized. Nothing is said about going down into the water;—of being buried with Christ in the watery grave; which surely would not have been omitted, had the apostles and the narrator of this transaction held to immersion as the only mode of baptism, and attached as much importance to the mode, as some at the present day. Lydia and her household were baptized, and there is nothing in the account of their baptism which implies that they were baptized by immersion, rather than by affusion, or sprinkling.

The next case is that of the jailer and family, the account of which is contained in the same chapter with the above, Paul and Silas, continuing at Philippi, were, at length, thrown into prison, and after "many stripes" had been "laid upon them," at the command of the magistrates, the jailer was strictly charged "to keep them safely;" who "thrust them into the inner prison, and made their feet fast in the stocks." "At midnight" they "prayed and sang praises unto God:"—the earthquake followed—the doors of the prison were thrown open—and the jailer drew his sword for the purpose of taking his own life, supposing that the prisoners had been fled; but Paul said, "Do thyself no harm, for we are all here. Then he called for a light, and sprang in, and came trembling, and fell down before Paul and Silas; and brought them out, and said, Sirs, what must I do to be saved? And they said, Believe on the Lord Jesus Christ, and thou shalt be saved, and thy house. And he took them the same hour of the night, and washed their stripes; and was baptized, he and all his straightway. And when he had brought them into his house, he set meat before them, and rejoiced, believing in God with all his house. And when it was day, the magistrates sent the sergeants, saying, Let those men go." All the circumstances in this case, make the supposition that the jailer and his family were immersed, preposterous. The supposition which the advocates for immersion sometimes make, that there was a bath in the prison adapted to this purpose, is without any foundation. And did they go away to the river at midnight, sore as they were by the former day's beating? And did they act so much the hypocrite, as to refuse to stir a step out of the prison in the morning, when the magistrates sent to let them go, when they had been away to the river during the night? It is said indeed that the jailer brought them out. This can mean only that he brought them out of the inner prison, to another part of it, where they preached to the jailer and his family the gospel,—and where the jailer washed their stripes,—and was baptized, he and all his straightway. Afterward the jailer brought them from this part of the prison to that portion of the building occupied by himself and family, and set meat before them. This is all the motion that the narration necessarily supposes, except that after their refreshment they probably returned to some other part of the prison, though it is not mentioned. But in this account, there is nothing that makes the most remote allusion to going out for immersion. Evidently Paul and Silas wrere much lacerated by the stripes which they had received, and their stripes needed to be washed and mollified to render them comfortable; they were evidently in an unfit state to go into the water. Look at all the circumstances, and then believe, if you can, that these were baptized by immersion. The man a jailer, whose life depended upon the security of the prisoners—his family—he having received a strict charge to keep his prisoners safely—the condition of Paul and Silas, exceedingly sore from the beating they had received—their unwillingness to leave the prison in the morning, even at the request of the magistrates— and, above all, the time of night, at midnight—all show us that there could have been no immersion in this case; and that they could have been baptized in no other way than by affusion or sprinkling.

The only other case of baptism mentioned, is that of certain disciples whom Paul found at Ephesus, as mentioned in Acts xix. 5. Paul inquired of them whether they had received the Holy Ghost. They answered, that they had not "heard whether there were any Holy Ghost." He said unto them, "Unto what then were ye baptized? And they said, Unto John's baptism." After being instructed by Paul, "they were baptized in the name of the Lord Jesus." This account shows that Paul did not consider John's baptism

Christian baptism,— for in this case he re-baptized those who had been baptized by, John. Nothing is said which goes in any degree to render it probable that these disciples were baptized by immersion, or that they were not baptized by sprinkling; for there are no circumstances giving any clue as to the mode in which they were baptized: it must be learned, if learned at all, from some other source.

The above nine cases are all that are mentioned in the New Testament, after the giving of the commission to baptize by Christ Jesus; only that Paul in his first epistle to the Corinthians mentions his having baptized Crispus and Gaius, and the household of Stephanus. In the whole history of all these cases, there is not a single circumstance mentioned, which shows that there was necessarily a case of immersion—and all the circumstances, every one of them, can be as easily reconciled with the mode of baptism by sprinkling, as by any other—and some of them are irreconcilable with the practice of immersion, and can be reconciled only with that of affusion or sprinkling; and show conclusively that either sprinkling or affusion, or both, were modes of baptizing with the apostles. Here it may be observed, as a very strange fact, if the apostles baptized by immersion, that, in all the cases of baptism mentioned, there is no intimation whatever of any movement from the place where they were for the purpose of baptism: such a thing could hardly have been. Even the case of the eunuch is not an exception to this fact. He only descended from the chariot to some water that happened to be at hand. Nor does it appear that in more than one case, that of Lydia, there was any water at hand convenient for immersion.

Now, I say, it is very singular, if there was all that going to and returning from the water, which would have been necessary, in case the apostles uniformly baptized by immersion, that it should not have been mentioned, nay, not even alluded to, in a single instance. And if the apostles attached that importance to the mode of baptism attached to it by some at the present day, that they should not on some occasion have spoken definitely of the mode in which they administered the ordinance.

Again, it is singular, if the apostles attached such importance to the mode of baptism, that of the multitudes of cases of the administration of the ordinance that must have taken place in the days of the apostles, the subject should have been mentioned only in so very small a number of cases, and in no case describing the mode in which administered. And had this importance concerning the mode existed in their minds, and especially did it exist in the mind of the Spirit by whose inspiration they wrote for the instruction of mankind, is it not certain that it would at least, in one single case have been so described, with all that definiteness and minuteness, as that all men desirous of knowing the truth, might as surely find the doctrine of immersion in the Bible, as that of repentance, or that of faith, or any other essential truth?

In my remarks I have exhibited the word *baptizo* as used in certain cases in the New Testament, and have shown that it does not always mean to immerse the whole body, and does not necessarily imply that in any case in which it is used. That *baptizo* means only and always to immerse the whole body, is the strong argument of many in favor of immersion. *Baptizo*, say they, has only one meaning, and that one meaning is, to immerse— and that to baptize is to immerse the whole body; but if this view of the subject be not sustained, the whole fabric falls to the ground. We- admit that *baptizo* has among its meanings, "to immerse," and Paedobaptist writers are quoted to show that it has such a meaning, and that therefore Paedobaptist writers sustain their views; but for this purpose, it ought to be shown that Paedobaptists admit that *baptizo* signifies not only to irnrnerse, but that it means that and nothing else. But this cannot be proved. Nor has it been proved that it means to immerse in a single instance in which it is used in the New Testament. For the word, as all Greek lexicographers say, means to wash, to tinge or die, to pour, and to sprinkle. Even Homer, the Greek classic poet, who lived a thousand years before Christ, describing a battle in a lake between a frog and a mouse, in which the mouse was killed, says, "that the lake was [ebaptisthe] baptized with the blood of the mouse," that is, was sprinkled or tinged in a small portion of it with the blood. I have shown that *baptizo* is used in reference to washing the hands; and that Paul includes sprinkling in the meaning of the word *baptismos*, baptism. And I have shown that other words that never properly signify immersion, are used to signify the rite of baptism; that John's baptism was not Christian baptism, Christian baptism not having then been introduced. And that Christ Jesus was not baptized as an example to his disciples, but to fulfil a law of righteousness pertaining to his office as High Priest. And I have shown that all the circumstances in relation to those cases of baptism mentioned in the New Testament as having taken place after the commission of Christ to his disciples, as contained in the text, may be as well applied to sprinkling as the mode of administration, as to immersion, and that in some cases, the idea of immersion is irreconcilable with the circumstances mentioned, or that immersion was impracticable. While, therefore, we admit that immersion is baptism, and do not intend to deny to any the right of their preferences; yet, we by no means admit that it is the only mode in which baptism can be administered consistently with the divine command; because we believe that baptism means the application of water to the subject in the name of the Father, and of the Son, and of the Holy Ghost.

But little of the direct evidence in favor of the mode which we have adopted, has been brought forward, and must be deferred till another opportunity. That there is in the Bible much to show that affusion or sprinkling is a proper and scriptural mode of administering the ordinance of baptism, and that there is much evidence aside from the Scriptures in favor of this mode, and that sprinkling is in accordance with the meaning of the word *baptizo*, and that this word was never supposed to have only the exclusive meaning which is by some given to it, until within a comparatively recent period, I shall attempt to show at another time; and conclude by the single remark, that it is of immensely greater importance to us that we have been baptized of the Holy Ghost, than that we have been outwardly baptized in this or that mode. Whether we are admitted to heaven or not will not depend upon the fact, whether in baptism we were immersed or sprinkled, but upon this, whether or not we have been born of God—have been "born of the Spirit,"— have become "dead unto sin," and "alive unto God," through our Lord Jesus Christ, —that we "put off the old man with his deeds, and put on the new man, which after God, is created anew in righteousness and true holiness," and "walk not after the flesh, but after the Spirit," "in newness of life;" for in Christ Jesus neither circumcision availeth any thing, nor uncircumcision, but a new creature." Let not then, brethren, our peculiarity be the zeal with which we pursue party distinctions; but the zeal with which we seek the glory of God, and maintain the great essential principles of the gospel of the grace of God, rather than those peculiarities by which we are known as a denomination. And in the principles of our church fellowship, let us endeavor to extend them as broad as the great Head of the church has done; that in all things we may be governed by love; and that we seek as the great end of our labors, the promotion of piety and godliness among men, by which, principally, Christ is glorified in us and by us.

THE MODE OF BAPTISM

—PART TWO—

DISCOURSES III AND IV

"Go ye therefore and teach all nations, baptizing them in the name of the Father, and of the Son, and of the Holy Ghost." —Matthew 28:19

In the previous chapter, concerning these words, I have shown that the word *baptizo* does not, as is frequently asserted, always mean to immerse the whole body; and that it is used in relation to the application of water, when only the hands were wet; and that Paul includes sprinkling in his diaphorois baptismois, divers baptisms—rendered divers washings; and that in no case in which *baptizo* is used in relation to the application of water to the human body, whether in baptism as a religious rite or otherwise, does it necessarily imply immersion. I have also shown that *baptismos*, baptism, is used in relation to the cleansing of things, which it is impossible should have been immersed, as the baptism of tables. Also, that John's baptism was not

Christian baptism, having been commenced and finished a
year and a half before Christian baptism was instituted, or
even known to the world; that Christ Jesus was not baptized
as an example for his followers, but to fulfil an existing
law of Moses, relating to the manner of introducing the
priests to their office, on the same principle on which he had
before been circumcised. And I have supposed it manifest
to every reflecting mind, that, if Christ had intended that
immersion should be essential to the validity of Christian
baptism, and the existence of a visible church on the earth,
he would, most certainly, some where, or some how, have
pointed out that mode so clearly and so definitely as that all
men might as easily find it, and be sure that they find it, as
they can find the duties of repentance, faith, and holiness in
the Bible. 1 have also shown that there is no evidence from
any of those cases in which water baptism is mentioned,
from any of the attending circumstances, that *baptizo*, to
baptize, or *baptisma* and *baptismos*, baptism, must mean
the immersion or dipping of the whole body; but that in
repeated instances such were the circumstances as rendered
immersion altogether impracticable. Also that in all the
cases where baptism was administered by the apostles, there
is no evidence in any single case that it was by immersion;
that numbers of them could not have been; and they have
said nothing in their account of baptisms administered
by them, from which we can infer, that they understood
baptism to mean immersion; or that they attached supreme
importance to the mode of baptism.

I next proceed to the consideration of some other things
supposed to favor the practice of immersion; and on the
supposition that *baptizo* always means to immerse, it may
be seen how very absurdly the Bible would read should we

always render this word to immerse. I now pass the more direct evidence in support of the mode which we have adopted, that is, sprinkling.

I proceed in the first place to consider those incidental expressions of Scripture which are supposed to favor the idea or practice of immersion.

Romans vi. 3, 4, and Col. ii. 12, are often brought forward as proof, that, by the apostles, baptism was always administered by immersion. The first of these passages is as follows: "Know ye not that so many of us as were baptized into Jesus Christ, were baptized into his death? Therefore we are buried with him by baptism into death: that like as Christ was raised up from the dead by the glory of the Father, even so we also should walk in newness of life." It is first assumed that to baptize is to immerse and nothing else; and then it is taken for granted that this passage refers to immersion as the mode of baptism. If we look at it again, we shall perceive that it can have no reference to the mode in which baptism was administered. In the 4th, 5th, and 6th verses the apostle uses three figures, or makes allusion to three distinct things, and they are all connected with the subject of baptism. The first, "unto death," alludes to the death and resurrection of Christ; next, to that of planting, in which seed is planted in the earth and there left till it spring forth into new life and that which is planted dies; and last, he refers to crucifixion, and undoubtedly to that of Christ, suffering death upon the cross, then rising to life from the dead, "that the body of sin might be destroyed." How can any person infer from these that baptism was designed to symbolize the burial of Christ, and not the act of planting, or the suffering of death upon the cross? Why also should it not represent the manner of his resurrection as well as burial? The apostle is evidently speaking of moral and spiritual death and resurrection. In baptism the person renounced sin, and engaged to be as one "dead unto sin," and "alive unto righteousness" or unto God. And the apostle, in the 7th verse, makes this general remark in application of the figures he had used. "He that is dead is freed from sin,"—then draws this conclusion: "Now if we be dead with Christ, we believe that we shall also live with him." By baptism we profess a death unto sin, as Christ was dead, as he that is crucified dies, or as the seed of corn that is planted dies—then again, profession is made of newness of life by holiness; as Christ crucified was raised to life—or as the corn planted when it dies, springs up into new life to bear fruit. This is the most that can be made of these figures. Unfortunately for those who adduce this passage as evidence for immersion, from the supposed resemblance there may be between immersion in water and the burial of a corpse in the ground, the apostle makes no allusion whatever to the burial of Christ, the disposition that was made of his body after his crucifixion, but to the simple fact of his death, and resurrection from the dead. The manner of his burial, or even the fact whether he were buried, is not brought into consideration at all;—it forms no part of the subject to which Paul alludes. But even admitting that the apostle intended to allude to the burial of Christ, how does immersion represent that burial? About as much as sprinkling represents the crucifixion of Christ. The burial of Christ was by no means such as they must suppose who introduce it for the purpose of proving immersion. Dr. Miller, in a late publication upon this subject, says,

> "The body of our Saviour was never buried in the manner in which we are accustomed to inter human

corpses, that is, by letting it down into the bosom of the earth and covering it with earth. It was placed in a tomb hewn out of a rock; not a tomb sunk in the earth, but hollowed out of a rock, above ground, and containing separate cells for the reception of bodies, 'as the manner of the Jews was to bury.' Even supposing, then, that it were yielded to our Baptist brethren that the design of the apostle is to teach the mode of baptism, by comparing it to the burial of Christ, it would by no means serve their purpose. There was not in fact any such subterranean immersion, if the expression may be allowed, as they imagine. The body of the Saviour was evidently laid in a stone cell, above ground, in which no earth came in contact with it, and in which, when the stone which closed up the door was taken away, the body was distinctly visible. In short, the burial of Christ no more resembled the modern interment of a dead body among us, than the depositing such a body, for a time, in an apartment in the basement story of a dwelling-house, the floor of which was either not sunk below the surface of the earth at all, or, if any, not more than a few inches, admitting of free ingress and egress as a common inhabited room. The 6gure in question, then, does not serve the turn of our Baptist brethren; thus affording another proof, that nothing more was intended by its use, than to set forth that, by being baptized into the death of Christ, we profess to be dead and buried in respect to sin, without any reference whatever to the mode in which either the burial or the baptism might be performed."

The body of Christ was carried into the tomb as you would carry an object into a room of a house by the door—it was above ground, for a great stone was rolled up to the door of the tomb—and after the resurrection the women came and looked in directly upon the place where the body of Jesus had lain, and an angel was seen sitting at the head. All then that could be intended by being "baptized into the death of Christ," was a profession of being, in regard to sin, as a body dead, and alive unto holiness.

Professor Stuart, upon this passage, among many other things, has the following remarks—

> "The obvious meaning of washing with water or immersion in water is, that it is symbolical of purity, cleansing, purification. But how will this aptly signify burying in the grave, the place of corruption, loathsomeness, and destruction? The apostle had in view only a burying which is moral and spiritual; for the same reasons that he had a moral and spiritual [not a physical] resurrection in view in the corresponding part of the antithesis. I cannot see that there is any more necessary reference here to the mode of baptism, than there is to the mode of the resurrection."

The passage in Colossians is designed to represent the same idea; death unto sin, and resurrection to a life of holiness, through the faith of the operation of God. Paul says,

> "Buried with him in baptism, wherein ye are also risen with him through the faith of the operation of God, which hath raised him from the dead."

As in the passage in Romans, no allusion is made to the mode of burial. His object was not to illustrate the mode of baptism, nor to illustrate any subject by the mode of baptism, but to point out what was professed and implied in baptism of a moral and spiritual nature. The same idea is expressed in the preceding verse by circumcision; where the apostle calls baptism, circumcision. He says,

> "In whom also ye are circumcised with the circumcision made without hands in putting off the body of the sins of the flesh by the circumcision of Christ."

There is, then, to say the least, equal reason why the mode of baptism should represent circumcision, as there is, that it should represent a burial. The meaning of all this phraseology is the same: by baptism, the Christian professes a death unto sin, and a life unto holiness. In regard to the meaning of these passages in Romans and Colossians, Dr. Judson, Baptist missionary to Burmah, says, in his Treatise on Baptism,

> "The apostle is speaking of spiritual circumcision and spiritual baptism."

And his conclusion is, that the apostle had no reference to the mode of baptism in these allusions. By spiritual baptism he must mean the baptism of the heart by the Holy Spirit. And it is to be remembered that baptism was not designed to commemorate the death of Christ, nor to symbolize the mode of his burial. The Scriptures contain no requisition of this kind. The Lord's supper is designed to represent the death of Christ; and they that make the ordinance of baptism symbolical of the burial of Christ, do it upon their own authority, without any command of Christ, and without any countenance whatever from the Scriptures.

Another passage which is sometimes brought forward, favoring, as is supposed, the practice of immersion, is 1 Peter, iii. 20, 21:

> "The long-suffering of God waited in the days of Noah, while the ark was preparing, wherein eight souls were saved by water: the like figure whereunto baptism doth now save us, (not the putting away of the filth of the flesh, but the answer of a good conscience towards God,) by the resurrection of Jesus Christ."

By what kind of logic any person can make out any likeness of immersion in this case, or of any mode of baptism, I am unable to conjecture. If the expression, "the like figure whereunto," referred to those that were overwhelmed by the flood, then I could easily conceive how it should represent a real immersion; but it seems to refer to those that were saved in the ark; and there is nothing, by which it appears that they were sprinkled even by all the waters of the flood; for they were in a good and substantial built vessel that was water tight, and the waters of the flood were beneath them, except the sprinkling of the rain above and around them. My difficulty with this passage is, not in understanding definitely what the apostle means, but in finding in all the circumstances of Noah and his family, the remotest likeness to immersion as the mode of baptism, or any other mode of administering the ordinance; and in what way it can be lugged in so as to give any support to the cause of exclusive immersion, it is not so easy to conceive, unless it be in the fact that there was a great abundance of water in the flood.

There is another passage, 1 Cor. x. 1, 2, in which the subject of baptism is mentioned, where they are said to have been immersed, because, I suppose, they are said to have been baptized—

"Moreover, brethren, I would not that ye should be ignorant how that all our fathers were under the cloud, and all passed through the sea; and were all baptized unto Moses in the cloud and in the sea."

If this were all that is written concerning this transaction, in the Scriptures, then we might, without much imagination, ingenuity or violence to the sacred writings, suppose that they actually were immersed in the sea, somewhat after the manner of Pharaoh's host, though eventually extricated. But if there was any immersion in tbis case, it must have been on dry ground: for in the history of this transaction, as given by Moses, who was in it "a principal part," they are said to have gone through the sea on "dry ground;" "on dry land, in the midst of the sea, and the waters were a wall unto them on the right hand and on the left." There is no great difficulty in making out all that Paul says concerning this event, in connection with the circumstances as mentioned in the Scriptures, viz: that they were baptized on "dry ground," on "dry land." I believe it was not an uncommon thing in Paul's day, for persons to be baptized on dry land. However that may be, Paul says that the Israelites were baptized unto Moses; and Moses says it was on dry land. There is, however, a very great difficulty in making it appear how they could have been immersed in water, or immersed in any sense, on dry land; but at all events this must be made out, or the doctrine of exclusive immersion falls to the ground, and *baptizo* will not always signify to immerse. It is an exceedingly difficult case, and requires all the ingenuity and power of invention, in the human mind, to make out even the similitude of immersion in this case, because Moses insists upon the fact, and Paul does not deny it, that they were all the time on dry land.

The difficulty of the case arises from this assumption, that baptism is, in all cases, immersion. Were it not for this assumption, no one would ever have dreamed of making out of this a case of immersion. But let us see how they succeed. They suppose that in this case there was a figure or likeness of immersion, by the walls of water on the right hand, and on the left, and the cloud over head; and this makes out the likeness of immersion. A person must have a very accommodating imagination to make out of this either immersion, or a similitude of immersion, were it all true. There were a great multitude, not less than from two to three millions of the Israelites, besides a mixed multitude that went with them, also flocks and herds, even very much cattle, all walking erect on dry land. The walls of water must have been at a great distance from those in the midst of the host; for it was no narrow space of the sea that was removed and the land laid bare and dried, for this great multitude to pass over, in so short a time as they manifestly did. And then there is no evidence that the cloudy pillar covered them, or stood over them, at the time they were passing between the walls of water. The cloud passed from before the Israelites, and went behind them, before they entered the sea, and stood between them and the Egyptians, and was light to the Israelites and darkness to the Egyptians. And there is no evidence that it moved from this position till the Israelites had passed through the sea; but there is every reason to believe that the cloud continued between the Israelites and the Egyptians, giving light to the former, and creating darkness to the latter, till Israel had reached the opposite side of the sea; for until they had entirely passed over, the Egyptians seem not to have been aware of what was taking place; then the cloud was lifted up, and they discovered that Israel had gone, and the way they went; and in attempting to pursue them through that way, the Egyptians were all immersed in the sea.

Now even upon the supposition that they make out by the walls of the sea and the cloud, (were it there at the time,) a similitude to immersion, it does not meet the case as stated by Paul. It is not the likeness, or similitude of baptism, of which he speaks, but baptism itself; and if baptism is in all cases immersion, then it was an actual immersion. And to make their doctrine of immersion agree with the apostle's declaration, they must show that here was a case of actual immersion; but then the declaration of Moses that it was on dry land, renders it exceedingly difficult to make out the likeness of immersion, much more immersion itself. The declaration of the apostle does not necessarily suppose that they were baptized unto Moses in the cloud and in the sea at the same moment, nor even on the same day; and if they were, the Scriptures give us no account of the manner in which it was done, unless there was a cloud that arose with thunder and lightning, and the cloud sent out rain, as expressed by Asaph in the lxxvii. Psalm. If the psalmist designed, as is probable, to describe the passage of the Red Sea, then the baptism was by the sprinkling of the rain poured out from the cloud, when the Lord led the "people like a flock by the hand of Moses and Aaron." At all events, it is absolutely certain that there could have been no immersion in this case, because it was on "dry ground," on "dry land." And this case of baptism proves a little too much for our Baptist brethren, besides the insurmountable difficulties of proving a case of immersion on "dry land;" because it proves, as we may have occasion to state more particularly hereafter, that all the children, even the babes, as well as the adults that were capable of believing in Moses' doctrines, were baptized. Upon the whole, I have thought it very unfortunate for those that believe in immersion exclusively as the only possible baptism, that the apostle happened to mention this case of baptism.

The declaration of Paul in his Epistle to the Ephesians, "one baptism," is pointed to by some, as proving immersion. Their syllogism goes like this: Immersion is baptism, (it is admitted so to be by Paedobaptists), and, There is but one baptism; so then—Baptism is, therefore, always by immersion—consequently immersion is that one baptism!

This may have a perceived ring of logic to some, and doubtless to the minds of those who use it, quite satisfactorily so. But it seems to me that they who can satisfy their minds by this mode of reasoning, of the truth of the doctrine of exclusive immersion, would find but little difficulty in believing that the Israelites were immersed in water, on dry land. But let us see if the same kind of logic will not prove sprinkling to be the "one (true) baptism." Sprinkling is baptism, and there is but one baptism, therefore sprinkling is the "one baptism." Here the whole meaning of the apostle is made to relate to the mode of administering the ordinance of baptism, while it is doubtful if the apostle had in mind at all the mode of administration. And even if he had the outward ordinance of baptism in view, there is a more important consideration in regard to it, than the mode; even the form as specified by Christ. If then he intended to refer to the outward ordinance, it was to assert that there was only one form of baptism;—that the "one baptism" was the application of water to the subject, "in the name of the Father, and of the Son, and of the Holy Ghost." There is no other scriptural, outward baptism, but that which is administered in this form, because it is the form definitely prescribed by Jesus Christ. But it is not necessary to suppose that the apostle had any reference to the outward administration of the ordinance of baptism. There is a baptism of more importance than this, and with which all are baptized who receive the "one Lord," and worship the "one God and Father of all;" specifically that spiritual baptism by the Holy Ghost, by which the soul is washed and cleansed "from sin and uncleanness," "purged from dead works," and "created anew in righteousness and true holiness." This is that "one baptism" with which the Lord baptizes all his disciples that come unto God through him; and by which they are sealed unto the day of redemption. The Father, Son and Holy Ghost, are engaged in the work of man's redemption. How much more rational to suppose that the apostle, when he had mentioned the Father and the Son, should also in the same connection mention the office of the Spirit; his "one baptism" by which sinners are cleansed and purified for the service of the Lord; than that he should descend to speak of the mode in which the outward ordinance of baptism is to be administered. But even supposing that he referred to the outward ordinance, what remote allusion is there to the mode. Men must be exceedingly pressed for reasons for their belief, when such passages are introduced with such arguments to prove the doctrine which they wish to sustain.

I have now examined all those passages in the Bible which are generally brought forward to sustain the doctrine, that immersion is the only valid baptism; and it is manifest that neither Christ nor his apostles have any where described the mode in which baptism must be administered, to be valid. It is seen clearly from the Scriptures, that the words rendered baptize and baptism do not necessarily signify immersion in any case where they are used;—that in the New Testament these words are used to signify the application of water to the hands, as in Mark iv.; and sprinkling, as in Heb. ix. as explained by the apostle himself.

II. *How must we understand the word baptizo?*

I now proceed to show, that to render the word *baptizo*, in all cases, to immerse, as it is contended it ought to be, would make ridiculous nonsense of the Scriptures, if not something worse.

A few examples of this rendering will suffice. John, the forerunner of Christ, speaking to the Jews of him that should come after him, says, "he shall baptize you with the Holy Ghost." Here let me turn the attention to the account which is given of the transaction by which the apostles were endued with power from on high, and received the gift of tongues on the morning of the day of Pentecost. "And suddenly there came a sound from heaven, as of a rushing mighty wind, and it filled all the house where they were sitting. And there appeared unto them cloven tongues, as of fire, and it sat upon each of them. And they were all filled with the Holy Ghost, and began to speak with other tongues, as the Spirit gave them utterance." This is said to have been emphatically the baptism of the Holy Ghost. So it is said that they were immersed in the Holy Ghost, which filled all the room where they were sitting. But is there nothing more than absurdity in supposing a room filled with the Holy Ghost, and the apostles immersed it? Is there nothing of irreverence in such an idea; in circum-scribing God the Holy Ghost to the limits of a room, and the disciples immersed in him? But however this may be, it is adding to the account which the inspired writer has given us. He says nothing about the Holy Ghost filling the room, or of the disciples being immersed in the Holy Ghost. It was the sound from heaven which he says filled all the house. "And suddenly there came a sound from heaven as of a rushing mighty wind, and it" (the sound) "filled all the house where they were sitting." By what authority do men make this sound to be the Holy Ghost, and then suppose the disciples immersed in it? Who ever before heard of persons immersed in a sound? Supposing a sound should fill all the land, as of thunder, or an earthquake, who would subject himself to the imputation of ridiculous nonsense, by saying that the inhabitants were immersed in such sound? And then sound is not the Holy Ghost. What then, is it asked, was this sound? Why, it was a sound—a preternatural sound from heaven, giving the disciples a premonition of the approaching fulfilment of the promise of Christ; of the coming of the Holy Ghost, by whom they were to be endued with power from on high— or at least, reminding them that some extraordinary event was about to take place. After the sound, the Holy Ghost assumed a visible appearance, and sat upon each of them in the form of cloven tongues. In another place, it may be shown how the scriptural account of this matter favors the idea of another mode of baptism than immersion.

But to show the absurdity of always rendering the word *baptizo*, by immerse, we have only to take two or three examples. Take the declaration of John the Baptist, as found in Matthew iii. 11; the same in Luke iii. 16, and render *baptizo*, immerse, and its impropriety will at once be seen. "I indeed" immerse "you with water,... but he that cometh after me is mightier than I, whose shoes I am not worthy to bear: he shall" immerse "you with the Holy Ghost and with fire." The same also in Mark, with the exception of the fire. John i. 33. "He that sent me to" immerse "with water, the same said unto me, Upon whom thou shalt see the Spirit descending and remaining upon him, the same is he which" immerseth "with the Holy Ghost." Again in Acts i. 5, and xi. 16. "John truly" immersed "with water, but ye shall be" immersed "with the Holy Ghost not many days hence." So also the remarks in relation to the custom of the Jews: "Except they wash their hands oft, eat not; and when they come from the market, except they wash they eat not"—and when they come from the market, except they immerse themselves they eat not. So in Luke xi. 38. "And when the Pharisee saw it, he marvelled that he had not first washed before dinner" had not first immersed himself before dinner. The above are sufficient to show that there is an obvious impropriety in always rendering the word *baptizo*, immerse; that to render the word in that only meaning, which, by the Baptists, is contended for, makes the most absurd nonsense of the Scriptures; and there appears to he something approaching blasphemy in saying that man is immersed in the Holy Ghost; and it is plain that the translators of the English Bible both understood the meaning of the word and translated it correctly.

III. *Baptizo does not mean "immersion" and only "immersion."*

I remark that no lexicon or dictionary of the Greek language limits the meaning of *baptizo* to the single act of immersing.[2]

Schrevelius, whose lexicon has long been one of the principal ones used in literary institutions, both in this country and others, gives, as the meanings of *baptizo*, "to baptize, to immerse, to wash, to besprinkle." Schleusner, "to immerse, to wash, to sprinkle, to pour out profusely." And there is no compilation of any Greek scholar, eminent for his researches in the language, that limits the meaning of the word to the single sense of immerse. And, says a writer upon this subject,

> "There is no one but that includes in the meaning of the word, sprinkling, washing—some to tinge, to stain, to dye. And besides, I have before me a multitude of Greek critics, all of whom include in the meaning of *baptizo*, to wash, to sprinkle, as well as to immerse; and this list

goes up to Tertullian, who lived within one hundred years of the apostles, who says that *baptizo* means not only to immerse, but to pour. All the ancients agree that the word has a variety of meanings, among which is always included the idea of sprinkling or affusion."

Even Mr. Carson, who strenuously maintains that *baptizo* means only to immerse, admits that he has all the Greek lexicographers against him.

Professor Stuart,[3] in his *Treatise on Baptism*, says,

"After a full examination of the meaning of *baptizo*, I do consider it quite plain that none of the circumstantial evidence," (that is, in relation to the cases of water baptism mentioned in the Bible,) "thus far proves immersion to have been exclusively the mode of Christian baptism, or even that of John. Indeed I consider this point so far made out, that I can hardly suppress the conviction, that if any one maintains the contrary, it must be either because he is unable rightly to estimate the nature or power of the Greek language; or because he is influenced in some measure by party feelings; or else, because he has looked at the subject in only a partial manner, without examining it fully and thoroughly."

Rev. Dr. Dwight, late president of Yale college, in his *Theology*, says,

"The body of learned critics and lexicographers declare that the original meaning of the words," (i. e. *baptizo* and its root, *bapto*,) "is to tinge, stain, dye or color; and that when it means immersion, it is only in a secondary and occasional sense; derived from the fact that such things as are dyed, stained or colored, are often immersed for this end. This interpretation of the words, also, they support by such a series of quotations, as seem unanswerably to evince, that this was the original,

classical meaning of these words. I have examined almost
one hundred instances, in which the word *baptizo* and its
derivatives are used in the New Testament, and four in
the Septuagint; these, so far as I have observed, being all
the instances contained in both. By this examination, it
is to my apprehension evident, that the following things
are true: that the primary meaning of these terms is
cleansing; the effect, not the mode, of washing: that the
mode is usually referred to incidentally, wherever these
words are mentioned, and that this is the case wherever
the ordinance of baptism is mentioned, and a reference
made at the same time to the mode of administration: that
these words, although often capable of denoting any mode
of washing, whether by affusion, sprinkling or immersion,
(since cleansing was familiarly accomplished by the Jews
in all these ways,) yet, in many instances, cannot, without
obvious impropriety, be made to signify immersion; and
in others, cannot signify it at all."

Dr. Miller says,

"Now we contend that this word" (i.e. *baptizo*) "does not
necessarily, nor even commonly, signify to immerse; but
also implies, to wash, to sprinkle, to pour on water, and to
tinge or dye with any liquid; and, therefore, accords very
well with the mode of baptism, by sprinkling or affusion."

In regard to the position often and confidently
maintained, that "the only and legitimate meaning of this
word is, to immerse;" Dr. Miller remarks,

"I can venture, my friends, to assure you, with the
utmost confidence, that this representation is wholly
incorrect. I can assure you, that the word which we render
(baptize,' does legitimately signify the application of water
in any way, as well as by immersion. Nay, I can assure
you, if the most mature and competent Greek scholars

that ever lived, may be allowed to decide in this case, that many examples of the use of this word occur in Scripture, in which it not only may, but manifestly must, signify sprinkling, perfusion, or washing in any way. Without entering into the minute details of Greek criticism in reference to this term, which would be neither suitable to our purpose, nor consistent with our limits; it will suffice to refer to a few of those passages of Scripture, which will at once illustrate and confirm the position which I have laid down.

Thus, when the evangelists tell us that the scribes and pharisees invariably 'washed (in the original, baptized) their hands before dinner;' when we are told that, when they come in from the market, 'except they wash (in the original, except they baptize) they eat not;' when we read of the pharisees being so scrupulous about the 'washing (in the original, the baptizing) of cups, and pots, and brazen vessels, and tables;' when our Saviour speaks of his disciples being 'baptized with the Holy Ghost,' in manifest allusion to the pouring out of the Holy Spirit on the day of Pentecost; when John the Baptist predicted, that they should be 'baptized with the Holy Ghost and with fire,' in reference to the Holy Ghost sitting upon each of them as with 'cloven tongues of fire' on the same day; when we find the apostle representing the children of Israel as all baptized by a cloud passing over without touching them ï and also as baptized in the Red sea, when we know that none of them were immersed in passing through, or, at most, only sprinkled by the spray of the watery walls on each side; for we are expressly told that they went through 'dry shod;' when Judus, in celebrating the paschal supper with his Master, in dipping a morsel of bread or a bunch of herbs in the 'sop' in the dish, is said, by Christ himself, to 'baptize his hand in the dish,' (as it is in the original, Matt. xxvi. 23,) which no one can imagine implies the

immersion of his whole hand in the gravy of which they
were all partaking; I say, when the word *baptizo* is used
in these and similar senses, it surely cannot mean in any
of these cases, to immerse or plunge. If a man is said by
the inspired evangelist to be baptized, when his hands
only are washed; and if 'tables' (or couches, on which
they reclined at meals, as appears from the original) are
spoken of as 'baptized,' when the cleansing of water was
applied to them in any manner, and when the complete
immersion of them in water is out of the question; surely
nothing can be plainer, than that the Holy Spirit who
indited the Scriptures, does not restrict the meaning of
this word to the idea of plunging, or total immersion."

IV. *Immersion was never considered essential* to the
validity of baptism till the Anabaptists arose in the
sixteenth century, a few years after the commencement of
the reformation under Luther.

They were called Anabaptists, because they re-baptized
those that had been baptized in infancy. Dr. Pond, in his
Treatise on Baptism, says,—

"I propose it as an indubitable fact, that immersion
never was considered as essential to baptism till the rise of
the Anabaptists (as they were then called) in the sixteenth
century. I say essential, for this, it will be recollected, is
the point at issue."

The Baptist attempts to disprove our views of the subject.
But how does he do it? Why, by proving that immersion
was practised in the early ages of the Christian church.
But this does not touch the point. We admit it. To make
their positions good, they should prove that nothing but
immersion in any case was considered as valid baptism:
for this is the question, whether immersion was considered

essential to the validity of baptism, and not whether baptism was performed sometimes or even generally by immersion. The early history of the church shows that baptism has always been performed in a variety of ways; by sprinkling, affusion or pouring, and by immersion. A few extracts from the early writers upon the subject, will suffice to establish this point. It is I believe a fact admitted, that the sick and feeble were baptized by sprinkling or pouring—and that on their recovery they were not re-baptized, but their baptism was considered good and sufficient.

Dr. Cave says,—

> "The primitive Christians did not hold sprinkling to be unlawful, especially in cases of necessity, of weakness, danger of death, or where conveniency of immersing could not be had."

He further says, that:

> "...they thought the martyrs sufficiently qualified for heaven, by being baptized in their own blood."

Mr. Walker tells us of a Jew, who, while travelling with Christians in the time of Marcus Aurelius Antoninus, about sixty or seventy years after the apostles, was converted, fell sick, and desired baptism. Not having water, they sprinkled him thrice with sand, in the name of the Father, the Son, and the Holy Ghost. He recovered, and his case was reported to the bishop, who decided that the man was baptized, "if he only had water poured on him again." This shows, not that such baptism is good, but that the primitive Christians were far from considering immersion essential to the validity of baptism.

Irenaeus mentions a sect of Christians who baptized by an affusion of water mixed with oil. Athanasius represents the Arians as administering baptism by sprinkling.

Cornelius, bishop of Rome, in a letter to Fabius, speaking of one Novatian, states that he was baptized in his bed—"baptized by affusion in his bed as he lay." "This shows that at the time when Novatian turned Christian, which could not, by this account, be much above one hundred years after the apostles, it was the custom for any one that in time of sickness desired baptism, to have it administered to him in his bed by affusion. It is true, the Christians had then a rule among themselves, that such an one, if he recovered, should never be preferred to any office in the church." [4] Because, as it was a little time afterward decreed by the council of Neo Cæsarea,—

"He that is baptized when he is sick, ought not to be made a priest, (for his coming to the faith is not voluntary, but from necessity,) unless his diligence and faith do afterward prove commendable, or the scarcity of men fit for the office do require it." [5]

Cyprian, the learned and distinguished bishop of Carthage, who lived about one hundred and fifty years after the apostles, in answer to the inquiry of one Magnus concerning the validity of baptism by affusion, said,

"You inquire also, my dear son, of such as obtain the grace in time of their sickness and infirmity; whether they are to be accounted lawful Christians; because they are not washed all over with the water of salvation; but have only some of it poured upon them. In which matter I would use so much modesty and humility, as not to prescribe so positively, but that every one should have the freedom of his own thought, and do as he thinks best.... The contagion of sin is not in the sacrament of salvation, washed off by the same measures that the dirt of the skin and the body is washed off in an ordinary and secular bath....And no man need think otherwise, because these sick people, when they receive the grace of our Lord, have nothing but an affusion or sprinkling. Whereas the holy Scripture by the prophet Ezekiel says, I will sprinkle clean water upon you, and you shall be clean."[6]

Lawrence, who died a martyr about 150 years after the apostles, baptized one of his executioners with a pitcher of water."[7] Eusebius also mentions Basilides as baptized in prison.... Probably this must have been done by affusion only of some small quantity of water. Because, as he says, the tyrannical jailers scarcely allowed prisoners the necessaries of life."[8]

Genadius, an eminent minister at Marseilles, in the fifth century, speaks of baptism as given in the French churches indifferently, by either of the ways of immersion or aspersion. For having said,

"We believe the way of salvation to be open only to baptized persons,"...."except in the case of martyrdom, in which all the sacraments of baptism are completed."

Then to show how martyrdom has all in it that baptism has, he says,

"The person to be baptized owns his faith before the priest. And when the interrogatories are put to him, makes answer. The same does a martyr before the heathen judge. He also owns his faith, and when the question is put to him, makes answer. The one, after his confession, is either wetted with water, or else plunged into it. The other is either wetted with his own blood, or else plunged in fire."[9]

Dupin states that Constantine the Great, being clothed with a white garment, and laid upon his bed, was baptized in a solemn manner by Eusebius.[10]

In the year 390, Aurelius Prudentius, a man of consular dignity, a Christian and a poet, thus sings in one of his evening hymns:

"Worshipper of God, remember that thou didst go
under the (rorem sanctum) holy dews of the font and laver;
in other words, that thou wast sprinkled in baptism."[11]

In the times of Thomas Aquinas and Bonaventure,
immersion was in Italy the most common way; but the other
was ordinary enough. Thomas speaks thus;

"Baptism may be given not only by immersion, but also
by affusion of water, or sprinkling with it. Bonaventure
says, that the way of affusion was probably used by the
apostles, and was in his time used in the churches of
France and some others."[12]

Similar quotations might be made in regard to every age
of the church, and there will be found none, till the 16th
century, who affirmed that immersion was necessary to the
validity of baptism.

Cyprian, the excellent bishop of Carthage, who lived
about 150 years after the apostles, could not take it upon
himself to say that immersion was the only valid baptism,
but on the contrary, quotes the declaration of the prophet
Ezekiel, saying, "Then will I sprinkle clean water upon
you, and ye shall be clean," as establishing the validity
of the baptism of those who were baptized by sprinkling
or affusion. History, then, shows us that baptism was in
the early ages of the church performed by sprinkling,
and pouring or affusion, as well as by immersion; and
that within a short period of the times of the apostles.
And how do those who hold to exclusive immersion meet
this historical testimony? They show from history, that,
in the early ages of the church, baptism was performed
by immersion; and therefore immersion is baptism, and
nothing else is, and consequently all ought to be immersed.
This is not the question, whether immersion was practised in

the early ages of the church. We admit it, and we admit that immersion is valid baptism. We again repeat it, the question is, whether immersion only was practised in the early ages of the church; and whether immersion was considered essential to the validity of baptism. It has been shown that immersion was never considered essential to the validity of baptism—and that sprinkling or affusion has been practised in every age, and was admitted by the most celebrated men in the early ages of the church to be valid baptism. Never was the thing known, that a person was excluded from the communion of the church on account of the mode of his baptism, till the sect, originally called Anabaptists, arose in the 16th century; and yet baptism, from the beginning, had been performed sometimes by immersion, sometimes by sprinkling, sometimes by pouring or affusion, sometimes by dipping the head thrice in water.

Dr. Wall, who had a partiality for immersion, says—

> "And on extraordinary occasions, baptism by affusion of water on the face, was by the ancients counted sufficient baptism. Of this there are many proofs."

The author of Letters to Bishop Hoadly, a learned and professed Baptist, admits, that,

> "...for thirteen hundred years successively after the apostles, sprinkling was permitted upon extraordinary occasions."

Mr. Robinson, also a learned Baptist, admits that,

> "before the reformation, sprinkling was held valid in cases of necessity."[13]

In the view of most of the Baptist denomination at present, there are no possible circumstances which would render any baptism valid but immersion. In this they differ essentially from the fathers of the church, that is, those eminent men who flourished during the first centuries of the Christian era, especially the excellent Cyprian, who could not take upon himself to assume that one particular mode rendered a person more acceptable to God than any other mode.

If the Baptists assume that immersion is evidently the scriptural mode of baptism, because generally practiced by the churches in the centuries immediately succeeding the age of the apostles, then the practice of those ages will prove a little too much even for themselves. If the fact that immersion was then practised, be authority for immersion now, then whatever else was then practised, will be authority for the same now; and this argument will prove a great deal too much, very many things which the Baptists themselves would be unwilling to grant.

Says Dr. Miller, Professor of Ecclesiastical History in Princeton Theological Seminary, in his *Sermons on Baptism*:

> "In the days of Cyprian, Cyril, Athanasius, and Chrysostom, when, as all agree, the mode of baptizing by immersion was the most prevalent method; there is no historical fact more perfectly established, than that whenever baptism was thus administered, the candidate, whether infant or adult, male or female, was entirely divested of all clothing; not merely of outer garments, but, I repeat, of all clothing. No exception was allowed in any case, even when the most timid and delicate female importunately desired it. Perhaps it will be asked, whether this fact in the history of Christian baptism is adverted to for the purpose of reflecting odium, in a sinister and indirect manner, on the practice of immersion. I answer, by no means; but simply for the purpose of showing, that in tracing the history of baptism by immersion, we have the very same evidence in favor of immersing divested of

all clothing, that we have for immersing at all; that, so far as the history of the church, subsequent to the apostolic age, informs us, these two practices must stand or fall together; and that an appendage to baptism so revolting, so immoral, and so entirely inadmissible, plainly shows that those who practised it, must have been chargeable with a superstitious and extravagant adoption of a mere form, which, from its character, we are compelled to believe was a human invention, and took its rise in the rudeness of growing superstition, perhaps from a source still more impure and criminal.

Besides, if the principle for which our Baptist brethren contend, be correct; if the immersion of the whole body be essential to Christian baptism; and if the thing signified be the cleansing and purifying of the individual by an ablution which must of necessity extend to the whole person, it would really seem that performing this ceremony, divested of all clothing, is essential to its emblematic meaning. Who ever thought of covering the hands with gloves when they were about to be washed?— or expected really to cleanse them through such covering? No wonder, then, when the principle began to find a place in the church, that the submersion of every part of the body in water, that the literal bathing of the whole person was essential both to the expressiveness and the validity of the emblematical transaction; no wonder, I say, that the obvious consequence should soon be admitted, that the whole body ought to be uncovered, as never fails to be the case with any member of the body which we wish to be successfully cleansed by bathing. And we have no hesitation in saying, that, if we fully adopted the general principle of our Baptist brethren in relation to this matter, we should no more think of subjecting the body to that process which must, in order to its validity, be strictly emblematical of a complete spiritual bathing, while covered with clothes, than we should think, in common life, of washing the hands or the feet, while carefully covered with the articles of dress with which they are commonly clothed. Whereas, if the principle of Paedobaptists on this subject be adopted, then the solemn application of water to that part of the body which is an epitome of the whole person, and which is always, as a matter of course, uncovered, is amply sufficient to answer every purpose of emblem and of benefit."

Concerning the fact of baptizing naked, Dr. Miller adds in a footnote, the following—

"The learned Wall speaks on this subject thus: 'The ancient Christians, when they were baptized by immersion, were all baptized naked; whether they were men, women, or children.[5]' "

The proofs of this, I shall omit, because it is a clear case. But lest some who hold to immersion as the only valid baptism, should deny this, let us hear what the zealous Baptist, Robert Robinson, says upon this subject,—

"The zealous Baptist, Robert Robinson, bears on this subject the following testimony: 'The primitive Christians baptized naked. Nothing is easier than to give proof of this by quotations from the authentic writings of the men who administered baptism, and who certainly knew in what way they themselves performed it. There is no ancient historical fact better authenticated than this. The evidence does not go on the evidence of the single word naked, for then a reader might suspect allegory; but in facts reported, and many reasons assigned for the practice.'—History of Baptism, p. 85."

(as quoted in another footnote by Dr. Miller)

Dr. Miller then quotes several examples dated in the fourth century.

Honesty in the Baptists requires, that, if they hold to immersion because it was practised by the early Christians, they should also hold to immersing naked, absolutely divested of all clothing, because that was as integral to the ritual as immersion itself.

It is often claimed that the Waldenses were Baptists, but without the least evidence, from their history. The Rev. Mr. Bent, of the Valley of Piedmont, the moderator of their Synod, said to Mr. Dwight,

> "The Waldenses have always baptized their infants and
> have done it by affusion."

Such is also the testimony of their written documents for centuries before the reformation.[14]

The mode of baptism by immersion is, to say the least, a very inconvenient one; and not a little indecent, even as now performed.

Although it may be asserted that there is no danger attending it, whatever may be the state of the weather, or the health of the subject; yet there is no lack of well-documented cases of injury arising from it; serious injury to the health, and in some cases, even of the loss of life in consequence to unseasonable exposure to cold winds after having been wet with cold water.

Immersion is in many cases impracticable; on account of the health of the persons desiring baptism, a lack of a convenient source of water in cities besieged and suffering drought, or in dry desert regions, like those inhabited by many of the Arabs in Africa. And man might travel hundreds of miles and not find enough water in which it would be possible to immerse a person.

The gospel is designed for the whole human family, and its ordinances are to be administered to mankind under all the circumstances, and in all places where they receive it. There are whole tribes of men inhabiting regions, where it is with the greatest difficulty that a sufficiency of water can be procured simply to maintain the life of man and beast, and where immersion would be for all efforts impossible: but these will all receive the gospel, and its ordinances must be administered to them. So it is also in the cold regions of the North, where for a great part of the year impenetrable ice covers all the fountains, ponds, and streams of water, and even the ocean itself. Additionally, in many cases of sickness or frailty, immersion is impracticable, without endangering life itself. It is often found that the dying person, under circumstances in which it would be certain death to immerse, ardently desires to make a profession of faith, and to receive Christian baptism, and to commemorate the death of Christ by receiving the symbols of his body and blood in connection with fellow Christians, in the ordinance of the Lord's supper. There was in one of our cities a very interesting and pious little girl, an account of whose life you may have heard. She was taken sick and brought down to the grave. Before she died, she became exceedingly desirous to make a profession of faith, and to commemorate with Christians the death of her Saviour in the ordinance of the Lord's Supper. Her parents were Baptists. She was visited by several clergymen, among them a Congregationalist. It was found, after consultation with her physicians, that her desire could not be gratified by her receiving baptism by immersion; her health did not allow it, and it was finally agreed that she might receive baptism by sprinkling; which was administered by this Congregationalist minister, and she became a member of his church, and the strong desire of her heart was gratified in commemorating the death of

Christ in the ordinance of the Lord's Supper in connection with her fellow Christians, as preparatory to her celebrating the praises of redeeming love in the midst of the church above. Say you that this was the childish notion of a little girl? Though she has for years been in heaven, I do not think that she has yet repented of it or seen folly in it.

Can a view of the mode of baptism be right, according to the mind of Christ, which shuts out from his visible kingdom, and debars from the privileges of the sacraments of the Christian religion, every person in such circumstances? I cannot readily believe, without positive authority, that Christ requires old and young, the strong and the weak, those in health and those debilitated by disease, male and female, in any case, if they would profess Christ, to be fully immersed, if it may only be accomplished through a hole cut in the ice, to receive a Christian ordinance.

These difficulties have been felt by many of the Baptists themselves; and many of them have renounced immersion. The whole body of the Mennonite Baptists, pressed with these and the like practical difficulties, consisting of several hundred churches, in Germany and the United States, have laid aside immersion, and have adopted baptism by affusion; that is, by having water poured through the administrator's hands, upon the head of the person being baptized.

Baptists evidently make the mode of baptism one of, if not sometimes, the single great essential of their distinctive religion. According to their view, without immersion, and only immersion, there can be no admittance to the visible kingdom of Christ. Since neither Christ nor his apostles have anywhere specified immersion as necessary to a standing in His church on earth—cannot it then be said that they "teach for doctrine the commandments of men?"

Again, in relation to immersion, much is said about being willing to obey the command of Christ. But Christ never gave any commandment, that we must be immersed. If he had, it would have been pointed out before now. Also much is said about being willing to follow the example of the Saviour, when he came "up out of the water." But why this stress laid upon following His example, even if his baptism had been a Christian ordinance, which the fact is it was not, or even if he had been baptized by immersion, (of which there is also no proof), the while the example of Christ in other things is entirely disregarded, as to the mode in which he did them; things just as important to be followed, as the mode of baptism? Isn't it obviously, as I conceive, because this is the point of their sectarian distinction—the badge of their order. The Lord's supper is quite as important an institution as baptism; yet nothing is said about following the example of Christ in this. To be consistent, why should they not insist as strenuously upon following the example of Christ in this sacrament? All admit this to be one of the only sacraments of the New Testament, and understand the manner in which Christ observed it. And as to the mode of observing this ordinance, they certainly know, that, in a variety of particulars, they do not follow His singular example. They are satisfied, like all other rational Christians, with preserving the design and substance of the ordinance, and keeping the feast in an orderly manner. But they do not keep it at night after dark, in an upper chamber; they do not practice it exclusively with unleavened bread, nor with such wine as Christ used; nor do they observe it reclining or lying down upon couches, resting upon the left elbow, as did Christ and his disciples. So I ask, "Why do they neglect to follow the known example of Christ in this ordinance by scrupulously observing all the particulars the Holy Spirit was pleased to detail in sacred Scripture?" Why not insist just as strenuously upon following his example in the one thing as the other? Why not require that every disciple should, at least once, go up into a mountain, and continue all night in prayer to God? Simply, because these are not things which distinguish and separate them from others.

Again, Baptists evidently lay a stress upon immersion, and attach an importance to it, patently calculated to promulgate erroneous views concerning the meaning of, nature of and efficacy of baptism. In a recent conversation with a person, then but recently baptized by immersion, the person imagined that by being immersed, an act of very great humility had been performed; and seemed evidently to be resting upon their willing performance of the act with no small degree of confidence, for the favor of God and eternal life. The person had been willing to take up the "dreadful cross" of being baptized by immersion, which was to his understanding, required in following Christ, and therefore God would reward such a deed with his everlasting favor. Afterall, if one is willing to be immersed—if they are humble enough for this great test of a right state of heart—it is sufficient to be saved. Mankind has always been disposed to make more of outward ordinances, than belongs to them; so they have to a great extent made their religion to consist in outward forms and ceremonies. From this disposition has arisen all that enormous mass of superstitious observances in the papal church, upon which millions are building their hopes of eternal life, instead of resting upon the atoning sacrifice of Christ, "the Lord our righteousness." So when an outward ordinance becomes the distinguishing badge of a sect, they are in danger of making it something more than an outward ordinance, even of substituting it for certain moral qualities of heart, of which the outward ordinance is only an emblem, and which qualities Christ has made essential to salvation. Their badge must be held up to the public mind, and such an importance attached to it, as shall lead people to adopt it, for the purpose of preserving and enlarging the sect of which it seeks to promote. And how many will be likely to mistake the badge as the essential principle of the order? Otherwise, why do Baptists frequently, in times of revival of religion, press upon the attention of sinners laboring under the conviction of their sin, and borne down with the weight of their guilt; feeling that they are lost, and inquiring what they shall do to be saved, the subject of all things—immersion? Isn't it clearly that they feel that there is something intrinsic to the act of immersion that will answer the inquiry of the sinner, and remove the burden of his guilt, and give them hope in God? Do they not so frequently exhibit the subject as to convey to persons in this anxious state of mind, at least the impression that whenever one shall be willing to take up their cross and follow Christ by being immersed, that God will grant them peace? Do not some say it directly? And is there no danger that with their views of the importance of immersion as the mode of baptism, they should substitute immersion for regeneration? Indeed this view of the subject has already been adopted by a large portion of the Baptist denomination in the United States, according to Dr. Miller, through the influence, as I suppose, of one Campbell.

Upon this subject Dr. Miller says,

"A large and daily increasing sect has arisen, within a few years, in the bosom of the Baptist denomination, which maintains the delusive and destructive doctrine, that baptism is regeneration; that no man can be regenerated who is not immersed, and that all, without exception, who have a historical faith, and are immersed, are of course in a state of salvation. This sect is supposed to embrace one-half of the Baptist body in the western country, besides many in the east."

This is the natural result of those views which they before entertained of the importance of immersion. It is only taking one step more; and saying, in direct terms, what thousands had been led indirectly to believe, by the manner in which the subject had been presented to their minds—the all-absorbing and important subject of immersion; or in other words, this is the proper result of their former instructions: not that their teachers meant it so.

From these considerations, it is plainly manifest to my mind, that neither Christ nor his apostles have done or said anything, which warrants the conclusion that baptism by immersion is the only true Christian baptism. Nor do the Scriptures anywhere attach such an importance to the mode of baptism, as exclusive immersionists attach to it, nor do they anywhere designate a singularly valid mode. And also, it appears that no such importance was ever attached to the mode of baptism in the church, till the sect originally called Anabaptists, arose in the sixteenth century. We are sure that sprinkling has been practiced from the beginning; and that there are numbers of cases of baptism mentioned in the Scriptures, where any mode other than sprinkling or affusion was impracticable.

And now I proceed to offer, in addition to what has necessarily been already brought to view, our reasons, in a condensed form, for the mode which we have adopted.

Baptism is the application of water to the person baptized. It is administered in the name of the Father, and of the Son, and of the Holy Ghost. It signifies cleansing, purifying—and represents the inward cleansing or purifying of the heart from sin and uncleanness. A cleansing not in any way accomplished by the water applied to the outside of the man, but an inward cleansing by the application to the soul of the "blood of sprinkling", by the purifying and sanctifying influences of the Holy Spirit. It serves as a token of the covenant of God, and a seal of the righteousness of faith. Christ gave commission to his disciples, to go and teach, or disciple all nations, baptizing them in the name of the Father, and of the Son, and of the Holy Ghost.

I do not pretend or contend that Christ pointed out particularly the mode we must practice; nor have the apostles done so, nor is there any definitive example in Scripture from which we must obediently derive a sacred formula.

1. It will be remembered that the command to baptize was given to Jews, who, when it was given, and for a considerable time after, had no idea that they were to preach the gospel to any other than to the Jews settled in different nations: and for about eight years they preached to none other. So strongly were they impressed with the idea that all spiritual blessings were confined to their nation, that Peter was persuaded to go to the Gentiles only after receiving of a vision from heaven. How, then, would Jews be likely to understand this baptism, a symbol of the purification of the heart by the Holy Spirit? Whence did they acquire their views of the mode of symbolical purification or baptism? Christ did not prescribe it to them. It was then, something which was evidently understood by them, else it had to be

particularly described. If then the apostles understood what Christ intended by baptism, they must have learned it from other sources than any instructions given them by Christ, either at the time of the institution of Christian baptism, or afterwards through some ministry of the Holy Spirit. It does not appear that he gave them any instructions as to the mode previous to its institution. Remember that these Jews, in their services at the temple, had been accustomed to symbolical purification rituals and washings, having reference to the purification of the heart by the Holy Spirit. And how were these performed? I answer, in almost all cases by sprinkling.

If any one had touched a dead body, and thereby became unclean, the Lord says,

> "That soul shall be cut off from Israel, because the water of separation was not sprinkled upon him, he shall be unclean." (Num. 19:13)

When a person affected with the plague of leprosy, came to the priest for cleansing with his two living birds, cedar wood, scarlet, and hyssop, the priest was required with the blood of one of the birds to:

> "sprinkle upon him that was to be cleansed from the leprosy seven times, and shall pronounce him clean." (Lev. 14:7)

Among the services which the high priest was required to perform, on the day on which he made the yearly atonement for the holy place, the tabernacle, for himself and all the congregation—

> "He shall take of the blood of the bullock, and sprinkle it with his finger upon the mercy-seat eastward; and before the mercy-seat shall he sprinkle of the blood seven times." (Lev. 16:14)

So also was he to sprinkle of the blood of the goat; and as we shall see, he was required to sprinkle all the congregation. Paul, in describing the purifications at the temple, in his Epistle to the Hebrews, referring to the atonement made by Christ, says,

> "For if the blood of bulls and of goats, and the ashes of an heifer, sprinkling the unclean, sanctifieth to the purifying of the flesh; how much more shall the blood of Christ, who through the eternal Spirit offered himself without spot to God, purge your conscience from dead works to serve the living God?" (Heb. 9:13,14) When Moses had spoken every precept to all the people according to the law, he took the blood of calves and of goats, with water, and scarlet wool, and hyssop, and sprinkled both the book and all the people, saying, This is the blood of the testament which God hath enjoined unto you. Moreover, he sprinkled likewise with blood both the tabernacle and all the vessels of the ministry." (Heb. 9:19-21)

These purifications were typical of the purifying of the heart by the blood of Jesus Christ, the atoning sacrifice for sin, which is called "the blood of sprinkling." These purifications were performed continually in the temple. All the Jews from their childhood were accustomed to them. And did they not understand baptism to be a symbolical purification, having reference to the blood of Messiah applied to the heart by the Holy Spirit, in his cleansing, sanctifying, influences? How, then, would Jews, under these circumstances, be likely to understand how water would be applied in an ordinance, which was to be symbolize purification by the Holy Spirit applying the blood of the everlasting covenant in saving efficacy to the heart? Had they not, for ages, been accustomed to see this very thing typified in the temple, by the sprinkling of water and of blood in their holy services? They did not understand that baptism was a "washing away of the filth of the flesh," but a symbol of inward purity of heart. Would they not, then, be most likely to apply this sign in the same manner in which they had for ages been accustomed to seeing this inward purification symbolized in those services designed to set forth things to come, and therefore apply the sign of baptism by means of sprinkling?

2. Remember that the prophets, speaking of the coming of Christ and the influence of the gospel, when the Jews shall again be gathered and grafted into the good olive-tree, from which they have been broken off due to unbelief, and when the Gentile nations shall receive the word of life,—state the fact, that then they shall be sprinkled,—and sprinkled with water.

Isaiah, in the lii. chapter, speaking of the coming of Christ and the glory of his kingdom, and its extension over the nations, says,

"So shall he sprinkle many nations." (Isa. 52:15)

With what shall these many nations be sprinkled if not with water? And what sprinkling with water except in the ordinance of baptism? In the ordinances of the church, this is the only element used by any denomination with which they can be sprinkled. If it be said, that it is designed by this language to represent the inward cleansing of the heart by the blood of Christ, through faith in that blood which is called the blood of sprinkling; then, I would answer, that this inward cleansing of the heart is most directly and happily represented by the outward emblem, when the ordinance of baptism is administered by sprinkling. The prophet Ezekiel, in the xxxvi. chapter, speaking of the general prevalence of the gospel, and particularly of the gathering of the Jews unto Jesus Christ, from all nations whither they are scattered, again to be grafted into the good olive-tree, or in other words, when they shall receive Christ as their Messiah and their King, says,—

> "For I will take you from among the heathen, and gather you out of all countries, and will bring you into your own land. Then will sprinkle clean water upon you and ye shall be clean." (Ezek 36:24,25)

These were prophecies with which the disciples were familiar; and must have been understood by them as referring to the gospel dispensation; and this sprinkling with water, as referring to an outward ordinance, otherwise the language is altogether unintelligible. Many seem to apprehend that a person cannot be cleansed with water, unless he is plunged entirely into it; but God thinks that the Israelites may be cleansed, so far as cleansing with water is concerned, by their being sprinkled with it. And there is no water used in connection with any service in Christ's kingdom, having reference to any kind of purification, except in the ordinance of baptism.

Must they not, then, have understood it as referring to the mode of Christian baptism, especially as they had been accustomed to see purifications, or baptisms, performed at the temple by sprinkling? If it be said that this is figurative language, having reference to the moral cleansing of the heart by the Holy Spirit, still there can be no propriety in representing inward purification by sprinkling with water, unless sprinkling the outward man with water is an appropriate corresponding symbol of inward purity. And in the church there is no outward symbolical cleansing, but in the washing of baptism. Then cleansing by sprinkling, is an appropriate mode of applying water in baptism, (the Lord being judge,) as fitly representing the inward cleansing of the heart by the "renewing of the Holy Ghost." This passage in Ezekiel, as we have before shown, was quoted by Cyprian, the distinguished bishop of Carthage, about one hundred and fifty years after the apostles, in justification of the practice of applying water in Christian baptism by sprinkling.

3. Sprinkling or affusion, as a mode of baptism, bears the most direct resemblance, more than any other mode, to the manner in which the Holy Spirit is given, whose operations are symbolized by this ordinance.

It will not be questioned that baptism symbolizes, or represents the purification of the soul, and our ingrafting into Christ by the Holy Spirit. What, then, is the natural and significant mode of performing this rite? Evidently that mode which most nearly represents the thing signified; and this is, manifestly, either by sprinkling or pouring. Now what is the language (modal) employed in the Bible, when the gift and operations of the Holy Spirit are spoken of? Is it by any phraseology that bears any resemblance or makes any allusion to anything like plunging or immersion? Never. The Scriptures speak of the descent and operations of the Holy Spirit in the following typical language:

"I will pour out my Spirit unto you."

"I will pour my Spirit on thy seed."

"I will pour out my Spirit upon all flesh."

"He shall come down like rain upon the mown grass; as showers that water the earth."

"It is time to seek the Lord, till he come and rain righteousness upon you;..."

That is, till the Holy Spirit come unto you like rain. Is it not then manifest, that there is a significancy in baptism by sprinkling, representing most clearly the mode in which the Holy Spirit is given, and emblematical of his purifying influences? And is this not what baptism was ordained to represent, and not either the death or the burial of Jesus Christ: therefore—

4. When man is baptized by the Holy Ghost, it is by affusion. Christ said to his disciples, "Ye shall be baptized with the Holy Ghost not many days hence." Those that hold exclusively to immersion say, that is the only case of baptism by the Holy Ghost; because they suppose that they can construe something like immersion from it, and because there is no other case of which they can. The idea that Christians are all baptized with the Holy Ghost, is held up even to ridicule; but we shall soon perceive that they are so unfortunate as to differ entirely from the apostle Paul upon this subject.[15] And this baptism of the disciples is described by the Holy Ghost coming upon them. So were the three thousand baptized on the day of Pentecost, when the Holy Spirit was poured out upon them. Thus was the company of Cornelius baptized,

"The Holy Ghost fell on them as on us at the beginning." (Acts 11:15)

So is every one baptized that is "born of the Spirit" into the kingdom of Christ, whether Jew or Gentile, all have "one baptism," by the Spirit of grace and holiness. Upon this subject, the apostle Paul has left us no room to doubt. He says, in 1 Cor. xii. 13,

"For by one Spirit are we all baptized into one body, whether we be Jews or Gentiles, whether we be bond or free."

Men may excuse Paul, but there is no contradicting the fact, that Paul here styles the regeneration of Jews and Gentiles, bond and free, by the Holy Spirit, baptism by one Spirit.

Peter also calls the pouring out of the Spirit upon the company of Cornelius,— baptism. In his rehearsal of the matter before the brethren at Jerusalem, he says,

> "Then I remembered the word of the Lord, how that he said, John indeed baptized with water, but ye shall be baptized with the Holy Ghost."

It is manifest that Peter now understood the prediction of Christ, "...ye shall be baptized with the Holy Ghost," as referring to the Gentiles as well as to the apostles, that they should be baptized with the Holy Ghost, otherwise his quotation of the above declaration of Christ, and applying it to the case in question, to justify him in going to the Gentiles, was without any relevance. This passage shows not only that the Gentiles were baptized by the Holy Spirit, but also that they were thus baptized by pouring (affusion)—and that therefore the word *baptizo* in large measure communicates affusion. We therefore think that water baptism by affusion or sprinkling is the most appropriate and significant mode of representing the thing signified by it, the baptism of the heart by the affusions of the Holy Spirit.

5. The apostles themselves have defined *baptizo* to mean sprinkling or affusion. So also, by implication our Lord, when he said, "Ye shall be baptized with the Holy Ghost," extending its application to the Gentiles, when they should be baptized by the Holy Spirit poured out upon them from on high.

This is true of the baptism by the Holy Spirit, as we have just seen it defined by Peter, as promised by the Lord. The baptism of the Holy Spirit is always and only described by either affusion— pouring upon, or by sprinkling; and this application of the Holy Spirit, both our Lord and his apostles designate by the word *baptizo*. Paul defines *baptismos* (baptism) to mean, or include in its meanings, sprinkling, in the case already brought to view, in his diaphorois baptismois, (divers baptisms.) In these divers baptisms, he includes the various sprinklings performed in the services of the Jews, when Moses—

"sprinkled both the book and all the people;" when

"he sprinkled likewise with blood both the tabernacle, and all the vessels of the ministry."

"For if the blood of bulls and of goats, and the ashes of a heifer, sprinkling the unclean, sanctifieth to the purifying of the flesh,"

etc.

This definition of the word, is seen in those cases where man is said to be baptized, when water was applied only to the hands, as in Mark vii. 4:

"For the Pharisees, and all the Jews, except they wash their hands oft, eat not, holding the tradition of the elders. And when they come from the market, except they wash, (baptize,) they eat not."

Therefore, in applying water by sprinkling in Christian baptism, we are satisfied that it is in accordance with the scriptural meaning of the word *baptizo*, with the intention of Christ and his apostles, and agreeable to the mind of the Spirit, who manifests himself in affusions upon the heart, and whose operations baptism symbolizes, when, by affusion, he baptizes the heart in regeneration, cleansing it from sin and unrighteousness.

6. In numbers of the cases of baptism mentioned in the New Testament, any other mode of baptism than by affusion or sprinkling was evidently impracticable; and the total lack of scriptural evidence of immersion in any case, leads to the conclusion that sprinkling is according to the mind of Christ. In the case of the three thousand on the day of Pentecost; in that of Paul, feeble, blind, and fasting—his eyes just restored to sight—as yet without food; but having been baptized, he took meat, and was strengthened—all evidently done in the room where he was; and in that of the jailer and his family;—in these cases, I say, any other mode of baptism other than by affusion or sprinkling was clearly impracticable, highly unlikely, and arguably impossible. And also it is a fact that in no case of baptism mentioned in the New Testament, is there any intimation made to suggest a movement from the place where they were to another, for the purpose of baptism. Where they were, when they believed, is where they were baptized.

7. The design of baptism does not at all depend upon the physical effect of water—and therefore, not at all upon the quantity employed, but on its symbolical meaning, and the blessing of God by the affusions of the Spirit.

It is not to wash away the filth of the flesh. It is a symbol,— a religious rite,— a representation of inward purity. If baptism depended upon the effect of water upon the body, then should the quantity be an article of important consideration. No external ordinance has any power in itself to communicate a blessing; but by the blessing of God, ordinances become of benefit to man, by the purifying influences of the Holy Spirit. Did the benefit of baptism depend upon the quantity of water, then most surely our Lord and Saviour, in his kindness, and in the fullness of his instructions, had informed us of the fact, and every one should have a scrupulous regard to the quantity. Did he esteem it necessary for the purpose of securing the benefit of baptism, (as baptism is an important ordinance in his church,) that the whole body should be laid under water, then, without question, our Saviour had explicitly informed us of it. But the benefit of the ordinance of baptism has no connection with the influence of water on the body. "But it is the result of a divine blessing on a prescribed and striking emblem; and as the Word of God has no where" specifically "informed us of the precise mode in which that emblem shall be applied we infer that the divine blessing may attend upon any mode of applying it:" wherefore we think that sprinkling or affusion answers the divine command, does all that washing with water can do to secure the divine blessing. Sprinkling with the water of separation, sufficed to purify the unclean under the Jewish dispensation. And our Lord has left us a lesson of instruction in regard to symbolical washings, when he washed the disciples' feet; in which he has taught us that a symbolical washing does not depend upon the quantity of water used, nor the portion of the body to which the water is applied. "Peter said, Thou shalt never wash my feet. Jesus answered him, If I wash thee not, thou hast no part with me." And Peter immediately caught the mania of making too much of it; and said, "Lord, not my feet only, but also my hands and my head." Our Lord at once repressed the zeal and disposition of Peter to overdo in externals, by saying, "He that is washed, needeth not save to wash his feet, but is clean every whit;" that is, in a symbolical washing, all the benefit is secured by the washing of the feet, that could be secured by the washing the feet, the hands and the head; it is not the abundance of the water, but the nature of the thing, as a symbol. So in baptism. It is not the abundance of water, nor the portion of the body to which the water is applied, that secures the benefit; as a symbol of inward purity, all the benefit is secured by the application of the least portion of water to the face. Wherefore, we deem it sufficient, if water be applied to the head in baptism by sprinkling, knowing that water cannot wash away sin, though there be used, with it, "nitre and much soap."

8. We are satisfied that sprinkling is a scriptural mode of administering baptism, because it fitly represents the effect of the blood of the everlasting covenant, when applied to the heart by the power of the Holy Spirit. It is the blood of Christ that lays the foundation for the salvation of the sinner. We are "justified through faith in his blood." And says John, "The blood of Jesus Christ, his Son, cleanseth us from all sin." And this blood is called the "blood of sprinkling." "Ye are come," says Paul, "to Jesus the mediator of the new covenant, and to the blood of sprinkling." Peter in the introduction of his first Epistle, says, "Elect according to the foreknowledge of God the Father, through sancti-fication oi the Spirit, unto obedience and sprinkling of the blood of Jesus Christ." Paul, in Heb. x., says, "Having our hearts sprinkled from an evil conscience." Now I can perceive no propriety in the use of the word sprinkling, in the above passages, unless it have reference to the mode in which water is applied in the ordinance of baptism; the outward cleansing with water, being emblematical of inward cleansing by the Spirit and the blood of Christ. And if there be no ordinance in the church in which there is sprinking as an emblematical washing, then I am unable to perceive

the propriety of the use of the word sprinkling in the New
Testament at all; for to call the blood of Christ the blood
of sprinkling, gives us no idea, unless sprinkling is a mode
of cleansing, which represents to the mind the effect of the
blood of Christ upon the heart.

9. We are satisfied with sprinkling as a mode of baptism,
because God evidently approves it.

I do not intend by this that he disapproves of other modes.
All I say is, that he manifestly approves of sprinkling as a
mode of performing Christian baptism. They that practice
it have the approbation of the King in Zion. Individuals
enjoy the light of his countenance, peace of mind, joy in
the Holy Ghost, and the triumphs of faith. They live in the
comfort of hope, and bring forth the fruits of the Spirit
in their life, and die in the assured hope of a glorious
immortality. Churches which practice this mode, receive
many signal manifestations of the divine favor as churches;
giving evident demonstrations of his approbation of them
as churches of the Lord Jesus Christ, recognized as such in
heaven, and blessed as such before all the world. He hears
and answers their supplications; he blesses the preaching
of the gospel in the midst of them; pours out his Spirit
unto them, and his blessing upon their offspring; revives
in them his work, in answer to their prayers; comforts his
people with refreshings from his presence; and gives them
all the tokens of his approbation, which he gives to any
people. Christ says, "Ye are my friends if ye do whatsoever
I command you." Now could it be expected that the Lord
should thus "bless her gates; "pour out his Spirit upon those
churches; go with their missionaries, and bless their labors
to the conversion of thousands of the heathen, if they,

both churches and missionaries, were found disobedient in regard to a very important command of Christ? Instead of enlarging herself every year as she does, the Paedobaptist church would, long ago, have come to nought, as her opponents these many years have been predicting; especially if churches of our order are disobedient, in such a sense, to any command of Christ, as to throw them out of all claim to a standing in the visible kingdom of Christ on earth. But as long as those churches which practice sprinkling or affusion, maintain "the faith once delivered to the saints,n in its purity, and that with devoted piety and godliness, they will have nothing to fear.

From these considerations, we are fully satisfied that our mode of baptism is according to the mind of the Spirit, and renders obedience to the requisition of Jesus. It is convenient, adapted to all climates, in every part of the world; to persons in all conditions of life; at all seasons of the year; can be administered with perfect safety and propriety to persons in all conditions, male and female; to those that are feeble, as well as to those in health; to the aged and infirm, as well as to the robust youth; to those that are lying on the bed of sickness and death, who desire to profess Christ, and to partake with his people the memorials of his dying love, as well as to those that are in active life. It can be administered by ministers that are in feeble health; that are aged and infirm, as well as by the robust and strong. But if any prefer a different mode of administering this outward ordinance, we do not object to them, because they follow not with us in this particular. Let every one be fully satisfied vin his own mind. We would make no more of the mode of this ordinance, than is made of it in the Scriptures. But because others have been thrown into circumstances by which they

have been led to adopt other views, it is no reason why we
should exclude them from our fellowship and communion,
while they maintain the essential principles of the gospel
plan of salvation.

While we are satisfied that God has given no doubtful
tokens of his approbation of sprinkling, as a proper mode
of administering the ordinance of baptism, by the great
and long-continued blessings which he has bestowed upon
the churches that practise it; and consider that mode right,
according to the will of God, significant of the thing it is
designed to represent, and answering all the demands of
the Scriptures upon the subject; yet we do not consider it
in that sense right, that every other mode in any measure
differing I from it, must be wrong, and in that sense wrong,
as to exclude those practising it from the benefits of the
visible kingdom of Christ on earth, from the benefits of
Christian fellowship and communion. In the administration of the Lord's supper, we, by the elders or deacons,
distribute the consecrated elements to the members sitting
in their places. This is our mode; and this we conceive to
be right. We do not therefore consider those wrong, who
receive the elements sitting at a table, as the manner of
some is; because we consider any mode right, that is decent
and:il orderly; so that the design and end of the thing is
fully preserved, and all its benefits are secured. So in regard
to baptism, any mode is right that is significant, decent and
orderly, preserving the essential design of the ordinance.
We have our views as to which mode, all things considered,
is best adapted to all the circumstances in which mankind
are placed, of country and climate, health, and sickness;
and to answer all the demands of Christ. Still we yield to

others liberty of conscience to judge for themselves. And we should no more think of excluding one from Christ's table, because he differed from us in his views as to the mode in which it is proper to apply the water in baptism, than we should of excluding; him because he differed from us in relation to the mode of administering the elements in the communion of the supper; or because he should differ from us as to the propriety of having unleavened bread, rather than leavened; or sour wine, in preference to sweet. We know that Christ blesses those that differ from us in regard to the mode of Christian ordinances; and it does not become us to set up our judgment against that of Christ, and exclude from Christian fellowship, members of churches which Christ manifestly owns, and blesses with genuine revivals of religion.

We condemn none for their judgment in regard to the externals of religion, if so be that they comport with our sense of propriety, decency, and the great object or design of gospel institutions. Our principal objection to those who hold to immersion, is not that they prefer immersion to any other mode, but that they make immersion exclusively Christian baptism; attaching an importance to that mode, for which there is no warrant in the Scriptures. They attach an importance to their views of the mode, equal to a specific command of Christ, declaring immersion to be the mode, and then require all men to conform to their notions; when immersion is no where prescribed in the Bible, as the mode in which baptism must be administered. Do they not, then, teach for doctrines the commandments of men? We do not object that any one should be baptized in such mode as he may prefer. If we cannot satisfy any one that sprinkling or pouring will answer all the demands of the Scriptures upon the subject, we assent that they should go where they can receive baptism in that mode that will answer their views.

Outward ordinances, administered in whatsoever manner or mode they may be, avail not to the salvation of the soul, without the inward grace of the Spirit; and with this, that mode which answers the great end of gospel institutions, and which is convenient and adapted to every country and climate of the earth; to those in health and vigor; to those that are feeble, sick and dying, and which answers the enlightened conscience, the mind of the Spirit, and so all the demands of Christ, avails to the salvation of the soul, and the glory of God. Here is secured the renovating influence of the Spirit, applying the blood of sprinkling to the heart, and securing the blessing of Him whose favor is everlasting life. No enlightened conscience was ever troubled in a dying hour, about the quantity of water used in administering baptism; or about the fact whether he had received the Lord's supper in the mode now most generally adopted, or reclining at a table on mats or couches, after the mode of Christ and his apostles. The conscience, in such circumstances, is always satisfied if the spirit of the divine requisition has been complied with; and the rnind dwells upon other and more important things, even those fundamental principles upon which the salvation of the soul rests. And I repeat it, that we are even now satisfied, that in our mode of baptism we answer all the demands of Christ; and that Christ has, for ages, set his seal to it, by the grace of the Holy Spirit communicated. Our mode is simple, yet impressive, and has itself been blessed to the conviction and salvation of some who have witnessed it. And here we are willing to leave the subject, praying that all men may so understand it, that there shall, on account of it, be u no schism in the body of Christ;" but that they who love the Lord Jesus Christ, may keep the unity of the spirit in the bonds of peace—and at another time we may, Providence permitting, consider who are proper subjects of baptism.

THE SUBJECTS OF BAPTISM

DISCOURSES V AND VI

"Go ye therefore and teach all nations, baptizing them in the name of the Father, and of the Son, and of the Holy Ghost." —Matthew 28:19

HAVING closed my remarks upon the mode of administering the ordinance of baptism, and shown, as I think, clearly, that neither Christ nor his apostles have instructed us that the mode is essential to the validity of the ordinance; and from the history of the church, that the mode was never considered essential by any till the 16th century, when the Anabaptists arose in Germany, a variety of modes having always prevailed in the church; that in the cases of baptism mentioned in the New Testament, there is an entire want of evidence that immersion was practiced in any instance; that in numbers of those cases, any other mode than sprinkling or affusion was impracticable; that the word *baptizo* does not signify immersion exclusively, and that it does not necessarily imply immersion in any instance in which it is used in the New Testament; that it used to signify the application of water to the hands, and includes sprinkling in its meanings; also that Christ does not consider the mode essential, or in other words, approves of sprinkling or affusion, by the blessings he has conferred and does now confer upon churches practising these modes;—I now proceed,

Secondly, To show who are the proper subjects of baptism.

In attending to a subject, it is important to understand definitely the point under consideration. The question before us, is not whether adults who believe, are proper subjects of baptism; nor whether it is proper to insist that adults who are in a state of impenitence, should be required to repent and believe before they can be baptized. All are agreed in this. It is not whether a people out of Christ, whether heathen or otherwise, should be required to repent before they can be baptized, either adults or children: upon this there is no difference of opinion. Baptist and Paedobaptist missionaries preach the same doctrine, and say to their unconverted hearers, "Repent and be baptized, every one of you." But the question is, whether household baptism is scriptural or not; that is, whether we are warranted in baptizing the households of believing and covenanting parents. Concerning this subject, a question or difference of opinion has existed in the church since the former part of the 16th century. Some say that the Scriptures do not warrant household baptism; others, that they do. In answer to the question of the propriety of baptizing the children of believing parents, they that reject infant baptism say, many of them, that the Scriptures require men "to believe and be baptized," (by the way, there is no such passage in the Bible, though often quoted as the express words of Scripture,) to "repent and be baptized;" and teach that "they that believed were baptized;" and that Philip said to the eunuch, "If thou believest with all thine heart, thou mayest," that is, be baptized. All such directions are manifestly given to adults who are capable of repenting and believing, and have no reference to the propriety of household baptism, whether such baptism is scriptural or not. No one ever questioned the fact, whether the Scriptures require in unbaptized adults, evidence of repentance and faith prior to baptism. The simple question is, whether what is denominated infant or household baptism is scriptural and right. We are fully persuaded that there is abundance of evidence in support of infant baptism: others think not, and suppose that baptism is properly applied only to believing adults.

We do not admit that there is any sufficient ground to question the point, whether the infant seed of believing and covenanting parents, or where one of the parents is such, are proper subjects of Christian baptism. Of course, I do not mean that this doctrine is not questioned; (and what doctrine of the Bible has not been?) nor do I mean that a person may not be an honest and sincere Christian, and yet his mind not receive the evidence by which this position is sustained; nor do I suppose that I shall exhibit the evidence in support of this doctrine, in such a light, that all will assent to it; yet we do not admit that there is any more reasonable ground to question the fact that infant baptism has been the almost universal practise of the church from the days of the apostles, than there is to question whether such men as Alexander the Great, Caesar, Pompey, and Brutus have existed, or whether they performed the acts ascribed to them. I am aware that this is taking strong ground in the case; but I trust that it will be fully sustained by the evidence in the case. But whether our minds will be satisfied with the evidence in the case, will depend not a little upon the rules of evidence which we lay down for ourselves; "the kind and degree of evidence" which we demand in the case. Judicial tribunals often convict and condemn criminals to prison and to death, upon only circumstantial evidence; when, if it were laid down as an established rule of court, that no man could be condemned but by positive testimony in the case, then all circumstantial evidence would be of no avail; and however clearly proved guilty by such evidence, criminals must be pronounced innocent, and the greater portion of murderers, robbers, and thieves would escape punishment, for they are generally cautious in regard to having witnesses to their acts. So if our minds demand such positive testimony in the case of infant baptism, saying in so many words, baptize your infants or households—or, children ought to be baptized—then the mind will not be prepared to receive the evidence by which infant baptism is supported, however clear and decisive it may be. And I am free to admit, that if it be required of me to prove infant baptism by a positive and direct precept upon the subject, containing the injunction in so many words, 'baptize your children,' I could no more prove it, than I could, upon the same principle, prove the first day of the week to be the Christian Sabbath; or that females have a right to come to the communion; how much evidence soever there might be in the Scriptures upon the subject. This rule serves those who reject infant baptism, in this particular case; but when they come to other subjects, where the rule is equally applicable, it is laid by. As though a judge, whose particular friend is to be brought before him for trial, should lay down a rule of evidence which he knew would rule out the testimony

by which the guilt of his friend might be fully substanti-
ated in the crime charged against him; and as soon as the
case of his friend is closed, should resume the business of
the court according to the common rules of evidence. Is
it then right to lay down a rule in the examination of one
doctrine, which, if admitted in the examination of others,
would leave unsupported doctrines by all admitted to be
true? Then it is plain, that we ought not to lay down a rule
in regard to the kind of evidence to be received in one case,
by which we are not willing to be governed in other similar
cases. Should we not, acting under the rule which requires a
positive precept in so many words, that little children shall
be baptized, and rejecting infant baptism because there is
no such precept, be compelled also to reject the first day of
the week as the Christian Sabbath, and forbid all females
coming to the communion of the Lord's supper? But this
subject I may bring to view again in another place; and
without further remark, I proceed to the consideration of
what may be adduced in support of household baptism, and
the objections that are brought against the doctrine.

The evidence in support of the doctrine is of two kinds,
scriptural and historical—

I. *Let us attend to the scriptural evidence in support of
household baptism.*

1. I will show that the church and its covenant are the
same now as under the Jewish dispensation, and that the two
sacraments, baptism and the Lord's supper, stand in the place
of circumcision and the Passover; that these two sacraments
under the two dispensations, refer to the same spiritual
blessings; and as families are included in the covenant
blessings, so of course infants, and that therefore it is the

will of God, that the existing token of this covenant (i. e. baptism) should be applied to the households of believers, unless God has somewhere prohibited it.

In the first place, I remark, that the covenant of the church now, is that covenant which was made with Abraham, confirmed with Isaac and Jacob, and repeatedly ratified with all Israel, and under which the infant seed, that is the males, received the token of it, and became members of the church.

This covenant made with Abraham, is a covenant of grace, and sealed to the people of Israel the blessings of the God of grace.

Many attempts have been made to prove that this covenant was merely a national covenant, and sealed to the Jews, and to the Jews only, temporal, national blessings; and that, when that people ceased to exist as a nation, the covenant was, of course, dissolved, and that all the blessings secured by the covenant forever ceased; and that a new covenant has been framed and introduced, under which the church now exists and acts, and receives her blessings. This position is zealously maintained, because it is perceived, that, if the church now exists and receives her blessings under the covenant made with Abraham, then the existing token of this covenant ought to be applied to the children of believing and covenanting parents. This would follow as an irresistible conclusion.

Upon this subject, Dr. Miller remarks,—

"I am aware that our Baptist brethren contend, that the Old Testament dispensation was a kind of political economy, rather national than spiritual in its character; and, of course, that when the Jews ceased to be a people, the covenant under which they had been placed, was altogether laid aside, and a covenant of an entirely new character introduced. But nothing can be more evident, than that this view of the subject is entirely erroneous. The perpetuity of the Abrahamic covenant, and, of consequence, the identity of the church under both dispensations, is so plainly taught in the Scriptures, and follows so unavoidably from the radical scriptural principles concerning the church of God, that it is indeed wonderful how any believer in the Bible can call in question the fact. Every thing essential to ecclesiastical identity is evidently found here. The same divine Head; the same precious covenant; the same great spiritual design; the same atoning blood; the same sanctifying Spirit, in which we rejoice, as the life and the glory of the New Testament church, we know, from the testimony of Scripture, were also the life and the glory of the church before the coming of the Messiah. It is not more certain that a man, arrived at mature age, is the same individual that he was when an infant on his mother's lap, than it is that the church, in the plenitude of her light and privileges, after the coming of Christ, is the same church which, many centuries before, though with a much smaller amount of light and privilege, yet, as we are expressly told in the New Testament, (Acts vii. 38.) enjoyed the presence and guidance of her divine Head in the wilderness."

It must be admitted that God has no where in the Bible stated, directly or indirectly, that the covenant with Abraham was to cease its operations with the national existence of that people; nor is there any principle laid down in the Bible, which, by implication, would involve such a consequence. And I can see no reason for the position taken, that this covenant did thus cease in its operations, but the necessity of the case, in regard to those who reject infant baptism. God has, in his word, no where intimated that this covenant contained or conferred only national benefits, and that all the blessings of the covenant would cease when the Jews should cease to be a nation.

That this covenant contained promises of temporal blessings, national prosperity, and the land of Canaan, is indeed true. And it is also true, that these blessings were removed from Israel when they ceased to walk in the covenant of the Lord their God. But that these were all the blessings conferred by that covenant, or that they were its principle blessings, is not true. The terms in which the covenant is expressed utterly forbid such an idea. Its chief blessings are spiritual, great, everlasting, and extend not only to the Jews, but to all the nations of the earth, as may be seen by referring to the language in which it is expressed in the Scriptures. Gen. xii. 2, 3. God said to Abraham, "I will make of thee a great nation, and I will bless thee and make thy name great; and thou shalt be a blessing: and I will bless them that bless thee, and in thee shall all families of the earth be blessed." So in Gen. xvii. 3-9. "And Abram fell on his face: and God talked with him, saying, As for me, behold, my covenant is with thee, and thou shalt be a father of many nations. Neither shall thy name any more be called Abram; but thy name shall be Abraham; for a father of many nations have I made thee. And I will make thee exceeding fruitful, and I will make nations of thee; and kings shall come out of thee. And I will establish my covenant between me and thee, and thy seed after thee, in their generations for an everlasting covenant; to be a God unto thee and thy seed after thee. And I will give unto thee and to thy, seed after thee, the land wherein thou art a stranger, all the land of Canaan, for an everlasting possession; and I will be their God. And God said unto Abraham, Thou shalt keep my covenant therefore, thou, and thy seed after thee in their generations." Circumcision was given as the token of this covenant: "And he that is eight days old shall be circumcised

among you, every man child in your generations." And
they that were not circumcised, were to be cut off from
their people. In the same connection, the Lord, speaking
of Sarah, says, "And I will bless her, and give thee a son
also of her: yea, I will bless her, and she shall be a mother
of nations; kings of people shall be of her." Speaking of
Abraham in Gen. xviii. 18, God says, "And all the nations
of the earth shall be blessed in him; for I know him, that
he will command his children and his household after him,
and they shall keep the way of the Lord, to do justice and
judgment." In Gen. xxii. 18, the Lord said to Abraham, "And
in thy seed shall all the nations of the earth be blessed."
Again, in Lev. xxvi. 12, the Lord says to Israel, "And I will
walk among you, and will be your God, and ye shall be my
people." Wherefore the Lord also says to Israel, "Be ye holy,
for I the Lord your God am holy."

As Israel was encamped in the plains of Moab, the Lord
assembled them all before him, and there ratified with all
Israel his holy covenant. In this transaction the following
language is used—" Ye stand this day all of you before the
Lord your God; your captains of your tribes, your elders,
and your officers, with all the men of Israel, your little ones,
your wives, and thy stranger that is in thy camp, from the
hewer of thy wood unto the drawer of thy water: that thou
shouldest enter into covenant with the Lord thy God, and
into his oath, which the Lord thy God maketh with thee
this day: that he may establish thee today for a people unto
himself, and that he may be unto thee a God, as he hath
said unto thee, and as he hath sworn unto thy fathers, to
Abraham, to Isaac, and to Jacob." Deut. xxix.

This covenant, it is declared, should be an everlasting
covenant. Sometimes an attempt is made to prove that this

covenant was to terminate with the Jewish dispensation, because the word everlasting is occasionally used in a limited sense, that is, does not in all cases imply endless duration; therefore the Abrahamic covenant ended with the Jewish dispensation. I cannot comprehend such logic. It would prove Universalism equally well. Readers of the Bible will have observed, that everlasting always means such continuance of duration as the nature of the subject or object to which it is applied is capable of, consistent with the purposes of Jehovah: thus the everlasting hills will endure so long; as the world shall stand. And the everlasting covenant of God with his people will continue so long as the church on earth shall exist, for it was established and ratified with the church; yea, it will continue forever and ever, even with the church triumphant in heaven, then God will be their God and they shall be his people.

Is it not most plainly manifest that the terms of this covenant include not only temporal but spiritual blessings? If not, then it is difficult to conceive in what phraseology a promise of spiritual blessings could be conveyed. What else can be the meaning of the language in which the Lord promised that he would be their God and they should be his people? So Paul understood the subject, and this is the very language which he quotes in his Epistle to the Hebrews, as that in which is expressed all the blessings engaged to the church under the Christian dispensation. And did it not include spiritual blessings in his estimation, when he said, "Abraham believed God, and it was counted to him for righteousness?" And was not Christ the promised seed? So the Scriptures abundantly exhibit the subject. The apostle in his Epistle to the Hebrews, referring to the children of Israel, says, "Unto us was the gospel preached, as well as unto them." Again he says to the Corinthians, "They did all eat the same spiritual meat, and did all drink the same spiritual drink; for they drank of that spiritual rock which followed them, and that rock was Christ." Concerning Abraham, Christ says, "Your father Abraham rejoiced to see my day: he saw it and was glad." Christ was the subject of the promises and prophecies of the Old Testament; so the Christian church is said to be "built upon the foundation of the apostles and prophets, Jesus Christ himself being the chief cornerstone." Wherefore it is said of Christ in regard to the two disciples that were going to Emmaus, that "Beginning at Moses, and all the prophets, he expounded unto them in all the Scriptures, the things concerning himself." "And the Scripture foreseeing that God would justify the heathen through faith preached before the gospel unto Abraham." This last is the most explicit declaration that could be desired, that the covenant made with Abraham, contained in it promises of all the blessings which the gospel confers on him that believeth. And it would seem that nothing but the dire necessity of the position which they have taken concerning infant baptism, could compel the Baptist brethren, for a moment, to lay it down as a sober proposition, that the Abrahamic covenant embraced only temporal blessings, and related only to the civil polity of the Jewish nation. The language used concerning it by the writers of the New Testament, looks very little like confining its benefits to the temporal concerns of the Jewish nation. Under this covenant the Jews saw the promises afar off, believed, and through faith entered into rest. Is there any thing in the terms in which this covenant is expressed, that savors of the idea of confining its blessings to the people of the Jews? If not, then it was not strictly a national covenant, though it included all the nation, and conferred upon them national privileges and blessings, till they refused to walk in the statutes and ordinances of the Lord. Does it not manifestly include all the nations of the earth? "And in thy seed shall all the nations of the earth be blessed." Does it not extend even farther, and include all the families of all the nations of the earth? "In thee shall all the families of the earth be blessed." The promised blessings of the Abrahamic covenant cannot be fulfilled till they shall be extended to all the nations, and all the families of the earth. That covenant then is still in existence.

Now what is the light in which this subject is presented in the New Testament? Do the apostles in their instructions, recognize the existence of this covenant, and derive motives from the blessings promised in it, or do they not? It will be remembered that they, and all the first teachers of the gospel were Jews, and that all their instructions for the first eight years, were confined to the Jews, and when there were, of course, no other Scriptures than the Old Testament, and no other "promise "than that contained in the covenant made with Abraham. Keeping these facts in mind, let us refer to the language of Peter as he was preaching on the day of Pentecost. He says, "The promise is unto you and to your children, and to all that are afar off, even as many as the Lord our God shall call." What else could Peter mean by this, and the Jews understand by it, but that the covenant made with their fathers was still in operation, and its blessings now proffered them on their reception of Christ, the promised seed? A covenant containing blessings promised to parents and their seed, and Peter now includes parents and their children.

It is sometimes said that in the Epistle to the Hebrews, mention is made of a better covenant; a new and everlasting covenant, made with the house of Israel and the house of Judah, not according to the former covenant, which was faulty; that the first had become old and ready to vanish away. What covenant was this "old" and "faulty" covenant; ready to vanish away? To make any thing for the cause of those who deny infant baptism, it should be shown that this covenant "ready to vanish away," was the covenant made with Abraham, and confirmed with Isaac and Jacob, and their seed after them, for an everlasting covenant. But evidently the writer of the Epistle to the Hebrews meant no such thing. Of this we are very confident. He has specifically pointed out what covenant he refers to. He says it was "The covenant 1 made with your fathers, in the day that I took them by the hand to lead them out of Egypt." This, as a covenant of types and shadows, was done away by the full introduction of all that which was typified in it. With this covenant he contrasts that which was made with Abraham, and confirmed in Christ promised, and now called a new covenant, as being renewed and confirmed in Christ, come in the flesh, with the seed of Abraham, even with all those that had the faith of Abraham. And in specifying what this new covenant is, he uses the very language employed, when the covenant was given to Abraham. "I will be to them a God, and they shall be to me a people." And the whole argument of the apostle shows that he meant, by the old covenant, the ceremonial law; and he refers distinctly to the services under that covenant, which in other places he calls a law, that he might draw away the Jews from the observance of those carnal ordinances, and from their trust in them, and lead them to the spiritual worship of God, to put their trust in Christ, the substance of all that was shadowed forth in that covenant or law. But that there may be no manner of doubt of the continuance of the covenant made with Abraham, and the extension of the covenant and all its spiritual blessings to the Gentiles, hear the apostle in his Epistle to the Galatians. In this Epistle, he has expressed himself with that definiteness, which leaves no plausible ground to question the perpetuity of the Abrahamic covenant. When he would guard the Galatians against the influence of Judaizing teachers, and save them from being turned away from their trust in Christ, and their reliance upon the grace of God alone, to put confidence in the former Jewish ritual, and in the outward circumcision, he leads their minds to the contemplation of the promises alone, as contained in the covenant made with Abraham. And why refer the Gentiles to Abraham, and the covenant made with him? Why call them his seed? Why make Abraham's faith an example for Gentile converts, if Abraham's faith was not gospel faith, and the covenant made with him did not include the blessings of grace and salvation? Why, I say, call Gentiles the seed of Abraham, if the promise to Abraham and his seed did not include converts of the Gentile nations? On any other supposition than that these things were so, the language of the apostle must have been, to the Galatians, not only obscure, but incomprehensible. And if the Abrahamic covenant is not the covenant of the Christian church, then the language of the apostle is very strange. But on the supposition that it is, his language is very appropriate, and sets the whole subject in a very perspicuous light. The apostle says, quoting the language of Moses, "Abraham believed God, and it was counted to him for righteousness;" and then adds, "Know ye therefore, that they which are of faith, the same are the children of Abraham. And the Scripture foreseeing that God would justify the heathen through faith, preached before the gospel unto Abraham, saying, in thee shall all nations be blessed. So then they which be of faith are blessed with faithful Abraham.... Christ hath redeemed us from the curse of the law, being made a curse for us; for it is written, cursed is every one that hangeth on a tree: that the blessing of Abraham might come on the Gentiles through Jesus Christ: that we might receive the promise of the Spirit through faith. Brethren, I speak after the manner of men; though it be but a man's covenant, yet if it be confirmed, no man disannulled! or addeth thereto. Now to Abraham and his seed were the promises made. He saith not, and to seeds, as of many; but as of one, and to thy seed, which is Christ. And this I say, that the covenant which was confirmed before of God in Christ, the law, which was four hundred and thirty years after, cannot disannul, that it should make the promise of none effect. For if the inheritance be of the law, it is no more of promise, but God gave it to Abraham by promise." In the above passage we have Paul's exposition of the Abrahamic covenant, in several particulars. In the first place he introduces Abraham to the consideration of those Gentile converts, as an illustrious example of faith for their imitation, and of course, gospel faith; next he determines that all they that are of faith, are the children of Abraham, and are blessed with faithful Abraham, to whom the gospel was preached; next he determines that the preaching of the gospel to Abraham was in the very words of that covenant he made with him, "preached before the gospel unto Abraham, saying, In thee shall all nations be blessed;" next he determines that they that are of faith are included in the promise of that covenant, in which the gospel was preached to Abraham; therefore he determines the fact that the Abrahamic covenant still existed, and that the Gentiles ("all nations") were included in it, and that the Galatians were receiving their blessings through the promise of that covenant; so he says the blessing of Abraham comes upon the Gentiles; then concludes that the law (or the covenant which God made with Israel when he took them by the hand to lead them out of Egypt) could not disannul the covenant with Abraham, that the promise of that covenant should be of none effect; and shows that the inheritance is by the promise contained in that covenant. All this seems entirely without meaning, unless the apostle would persuade the Galatians that the covenant made with Abraham was a covenant of grace, and extended its blessings to them; unless this were so, his arguments must have been to them, ridiculous nonsense. Why tell the Galatians that this covenant with Abraham was confirmed of God in Christ, and could not be disannulled, if it were not then the covenant of grace to the church? Why tell them that the blessing of this covenant extended to all nations, if he did not intend to be understood that they, the Gentiles, were included—and so all Gentiles who should be blessed in Christ? Why tell them that the law which was four hundred and thirty years after could not disannul this covenant, if it was already abrogated, and a new and better covenant introduced? Why refer this church of Galatia to the promise of this covenant, "I will be a God to thee and thy seed after thee," if the covenant promised only national blessings to the Jews? They were not the seed of Abraham according to the flesh, nor in any sense included in the Jewish nation. It is most clearly manifest that the following things are true, viz., that the covenant made with Abraham is a covenant of grace, and that the most important blessings secured by that covenant were spiritual, and not temporal and national; that the blessings of this covenant extended to the Gentiles as well as Jews; and that by the seed of Abraham the Lord intended all, whether Jews or Gentiles, in every nation and age of the world, who should exercise the faith of Abraham, "they which are of faith, the sauie are the children of Abraham." No language can express the perpetuity of the Abrahamic covenant more clearly, than that in which it is here expressed by Paul. It would seem as if it were written in these latter days, expressly for the purpose of confuting those who affirm that the Abrahamic covenant secured only temporal blessings, and related only to the civil polity of the Jews, and ceased with the national existence of that people. So clearly does divine truth refute every important error in spiritual things.

The apostle then proceeds to speak definitely of the extension of the privileges and blessings of the covenant under the gospel dispensation. He says, "As many of you as have been baptized into Christ, have put on Christ. There is neither Jew nor Greek, there is neither bond nor free, there is neither male nor female: for ye are all one in Christ Jesus. And if ye be Christ's, then are ye Abraham's seed, and heirs according to the promise." "Seed of Abraham, and heirs according to the promise" made to Abraham, which promise cannot be made of none effect. God never made but one covenant with Abraham, its promises were many times repeated, and often referred to by the prophets for the confirmation of Israel. And in all references to it, it is styled "the covenant," or "his covenant." Zacharias, speaking of it on the occasion of the circumcision of John, says, "To perform the mercy promised to our fathers, and to remember his holy covenant; the oath which he sware unto our father Abraham."

Peter, preaching the gospel in the temple after the healing of the lame man, says, "Ye are the children of the prophets, and of the covenant which God made with our fathers, saying unto Abraham, And in thy seed shall all the kindreds of the earth be blessed." There can be no propriety whatever in the reference which Peter here makes to the Abrahamic covenant, unless that is the covenant of the church under the gospel dispensation. Either the covenant made with Abraham is the covenant of the church under the gospel dispensation, or both Paul and Peter seem evidently to have been grossly mistaken. But we think they were right, and all those wrong, who deny their positions, and say that the covenant made with Abraham is void, and its promise of none effect.

What then is the unavoidable conclusion? Evidently this; that if the covenant made with Abraham still exists as the covenant of the church, then the existing token of that covenant must be applied in that extent in which it was required to be applied, when it was originally given; that is, to the infant seed of believing, covenanting parents; unless some direction, command, precept or apostolic example can be produced, excluding children from the token and blessings of this covenant; but nothing of this character can be found: therefore children are to receive Christian baptism. I believe that this conclusion is felt to be unavoidable by those who deny infant baptism; and fully conscious that they cannot bring from the Scriptures any semblance of a prohibition to apply the token of the covenant to the seed of believing parents; they therefore labor to prove that the Abrahamic covenant is abolished, and is not the covenant of the Christian church:—but there it stands, in the instructions of Peter and Paul, in all clearness of the light of the noonday sun; and not the shadow of a cloud, or even of a mist, can be thrown over it. Men who require a positive precept for all they do, should bring some positive precept cutting off the infant seed of believing parents from their relation to the church, and from the blessings of that covenant, and it will immediately secure the universal assent of those that believe in the God of Abraham, and Isaac, and Jacob.

Then our conclusion is, that children under the gospel dispensation are included in the covenant, and therefore have a right to the existing token of the covenant, that is, to baptism, and that it is both the privilege and duty of parents to apply this token of the covenant and seal of the righteousness of faith to their children.

It is moreover evident, that this covenant with Abraham is a covenant of grace, or that it included the blessings of God's grace, from what was implied in the token of this covenant, which was circumcision. It was not to distinguish the Jews from other people as a nation; but was the seal of the righteousness of faith, and that faith having respect to Christ as its great object. Of Abraham, Paul says, Rom. iv. 11, 12, 16, "He received the sign of circumcision, a seal of the righteousness of the faith which he had, being yet uncircumcised; that he might be the father of all them that believe, though they be not circumcised, that righteousness might be imputed unto them also; and the father of circumcision to them who are not of the circumcision only, but who also walk in the steps of that faith of our father Abraham, which he had, being yet uncircumcised. ...."

Therefore it is of faith, that it might be by grace; to the end the promise might be sure to all the seed: not to that only which is of the law, but to that also which is of the faith of Abraham, who is the father of us all." Here it is distinctly stated that the token of the covenant with Abraham was a seal of the righteousness of faith, and therefore a covenant of spiritual and eternal blessings; and Abraham is styled the father of them that believe, who are not of the circumcision, i. e. of the Gentile converts. It is, thus plainly manifest that circumcision was not a national mark to distinguish the Jews from other nations. And the promise of the covenant was made sure to all the seed, including, according to the apostle's exposition, Gentile believers. All this is said to a Gentile church under the gospel dispensation. It is also manifest that the same moral and spiritual character was required under the Jewish, as is required under the gospel dispensation. Then, God said, "Be ye holy;" now, "Without holiness no man shall see the Lord."

The Jews had, for about two thousand years, been accustomed to consider their children as included in the covenant of God, and to apply unto them the token of the covenant; and with instructions such as they received from Peter and Paul, they must have considered them so still, under the gospel dispensation, without explicit instructions to the contrary: and even then, the Jews, strongly attached to their customs and privileges as they were, would not have given up those privileges, and have seen their children thrown out, without much murmuring, and many complaints. And if the apostles rejected the children, and withheld from them the token and benefits of the covenant under the gospel dispensation, it is strange that there was not even a murmur or complaint upon the subject; no, not even from those judaizing teachers, who were exceedingly zealous for circumcision and the law of ritual service, and all their supposed Jewish privileges, and would even impose them upon Gentile converts. Had the apostles rejected infants from baptism, they must have had a controversy upon the subject, as they had concerning circumcision, and their judgment had been given in the case for the benefit of all the churches, and had come down to us.

2. The church is the same under both dispensations. God has had but one visible church in the world. This will follow as a necessary consequence, as the church exists and receives all her blessings in the gospel dispensation, under the same covenant as in the Jewish dispensation. But if, as the opposers of infant baptism say, the church and covenant are now entirely distinct from those of the former dispensation; then where, when, and by whom was this church formed? In what does the new covenant differ from that established with Abraham, and ratified with Israel? When, where, and by whom was this covenant promulgated? When, where, and with what individuals was this covenant established? With whom, and in what manner, and with what rites was it ratified? The Bible is entirely silent as to any such transactions. Baptists say, that the gospel dispensation was introduced with the ministry of John. Were these things done by John? There is no allusion to any thing of the kind in the Bible. Are they said to have been done by Christ? There is no account of his doing any such things. Both John and Jesus Christ lived, labored, and died in the church under the Jewish dispensation, which manifestly closed the moment that Christ bowed his head and gave up the ghost. No transactions of the kind are alluded to, as

having been done by Christ after his resurrection. None of these things were done by the apostles after the ascension of Christ. Facts, as they are narrated in the Bible, will show that it was even so.

Christ Jesus was born under the Jewish dispensation, and by circumcision, became a member of the Jewish church. He lived, did most of his works, and died in that church. He performed all the rites and ceremonies pertaining to that dispensation, from circumcision, to the washing at Jordan, preparatory to his entrance upon the ministry; and from that, to the eating of the passover on the night in which he was betrayed. As Jesus passed along in the work of the ministry, he gathered around him followers, but they were still members of no other church than the Jewish, and so they continued to be members of the church under the Jewish dispensation, so long as that dispensation continued. They were the living branches in the Jewish church—and without any new covenant or re-organization, they became the Christian church and began to administer the ordinances which Christ had appointed, instead of those which had before been in use in the church. It was not till after they had preached the gospel more than eight years, in the Christian church, that they understood that this church was to be any other than the Jewish church, with new outward ordinances; for, during this time, they did not understand, that God would grant "unto the Gentiles repentance unto life." They supposed the church would consist of persons pertaining to the Jewish nation; either Jews, or such as should be incorporated with them by the initiatory rites then in use, circumcision and baptism. For a long time, as is stated by writers upon the subject, "proselytes to the Jewish religion had been circumcised, then the whole family were baptized, men, women, and children."

That there were changes in the church, is admitted. It was "time of reformation," as it is called in the Epistle to the Hebrews. And the men who commenced operations under the Christian dispensation, viz. the apostles, never, as we are any where informed, received the initiatory seal under that dispensation: that is, it does not appear that the apostles ever received Christian baptism; Paul excepted.

A fact, which I do not recollect to have seen mentioned by any writer upon the subject, seems to me of some importance in illustrating the identity of the Jewish and the Christian church. It is this; that the ordinance of the Lord's supper was instituted in, and during the existence of the Jewish dispensation, and was first celebrated, in anticipation of the event to which it relates, by the disciples, while members of the church under the Jewish dispensation, as yet in full operation; and while they were celebrating the Passover, an ordinance pertaining to that dispensation; and the Lord's supper was joined with it as almost a part of the same. The Passover was a type of the blood of Christ to be shed for the remission of sins; and the Lord's supper was a representation of his body broken, and blood now shed for the salvation of his people. The joining of these things in one feast, showed that they referred to the same thing, and were ordinances in the same church; the passover from thence to cease, and the Lord's supper to take its place in the church till Christ shall come again.

All the promises made to the church under the latter dispensation, were made under the former. Then, they were required to be holy—so now; then they were promised temporal blessings—so now; then they were promised spiritual blessings, pardon, the favor of God, and eternal life—so in the Christian dispensation, only in the latter more clearly and fully. God's real and invisible church has always been one and the same, composed of all those who have believed, worshipped, and served the Lord, and the visible church has always included most of its real members, as well as others.

But, as if to put the subject beyond all question and contradiction, the apostle Paul has given us such a representation of the sameness of the church under both dispensations, as leaves the subject forever settled. In his Epistle to the Romans, 11th chapter, he represents the church under the Jewish dispensation as a good olive-tree, having its root in Abraham, and the Jews its branches. He says, "And if some of the branches were broken off, and thou being a wild olive-tree, wert grafted in among them, and with them partakest of the root and fatness of the olive-tree." What does he say? That this is a representation of the church composed at first of Jews, then of Jews and Gentiles, none can deny. Does he say that the good olive-tree, the emblem of the church under the Jewish economy, was destroyed, or that it first had its existence in the establishment of the Christian church? No such thing. But the tree, that is, the church established by the Abrahamic covenant, the good olive-tree, with its root and fatness remains, and the unfruitful or dead branches were cut away, and the Gentiles were grafted in among the remaining fruitful branches, and with them partook of the root and fatness of the good olive-tree. Is not the perpetuity of the church, or the truth, that the church under both dispensations is one and the same, here taught with all possible perspicuity? Is there any possible ground of doubt? Does not the apostle here contradict in the plainest and most absolute manner possible, the supposition, that the church under the Christian dispensation is entirely separate and distinct from that under the Jewish? And does he not assert in the clearest terms, that the Jewish church was continued under the gospel dispensation, and constituted the root and fatness of the Christian church; and that the blessings of this church are founded on the promises made in the Abrahamic covenant? Instead of representing a new church, under a new covenant, as formed at the beginning of the Christian dispensation, he states that the Gentiles became a part and parcel of the original church founded in Abraham, by being cut out of the wild olive by nature, and being grafted in among the remaining, living branches of the good olive-tree. Then, is it not certain that the token of the covenant and all its blessings extend equally to children under the latter, as under the former dispensation, since the church is the same church, one good olive-tree, formed in Abraham, into which the Gentiles have been grafted? Unless there is somewhere a prohibition that cuts them off, the terms of the covenant embrace the children of believing parents, and the existing token of the covenant, that is, baptism, should still be applied to them.

In this same connection the apostle alludes to a subject of prophecy, the restoration of the Jews, and says, "They also, if they abide not still in unbelief, shall be grafted in again; for God is able to graft them in." And to "graft them into their own good olive-tree." This most evidently means, that they are to be restored to the blessings of the Abrahamic covenant, from which, by unbelief, they were cut off. Jeremiah, prophesying concerning the restoration of the Jews, says, "And their children shall be as aforetime." Isaiah, concerning the prosperity and glory of the church, says, "I will pour my Spirit upon thy seed, and my blessing upon thine offspring." Again, speaking of the calling of the Gentiles, and their introduction into the Christian church, he says, (chap. lxv.) "They shall not labor in vain, nor bring forth for trouble; for they are the seed of the blessed, and their offspring with them." The covenant and the church being the same under the Christian as under the Jewish dispensation, then the token of the covenant, that is, baptism, is to be applied to the children of believing parents, unless we are forbidden so to do.

3. Circumcision in the church has given place to baptism; that is, the latter stands in the place of the former.

There is no question that the Lord's supper has taken the place of the passover in the church, and the church being the same under both dispensations, there can be no reasonable doubt, that baptism has taken the place of circumcision. They are both emblems or signs of the same thing. As baptism is a prerequisite to a standing in the visible church, so also was circumcision; as the latter was a token of the covenant of God made with Abraham, so is the former; and each is a seal of the righteousness of faith, sealing to believers the blessings promised in the everlasting covenant. Both point out the necessity of regeneration, of a new heart, and of holiness of life.

Dr. Pond, in his *Treatise*, in support of the position that baptism has taken the place of circumcision, says, they "are of precisely the same import. Circumcision, as a token of the covenant, was both a sign and a seal. As a sign, it represented the circumcision of the heart, or regeneration. 'Circumcision is of the heart, in the spirit and not in the letter.' Rom. ii. 29. As a seal, circumcision confirmed the; 'righteousness of faith,' or the covenant of grace. Rom. iv. 11. Such was the import of circumcision. And is not that of baptism precisely similar? This, too, is both a sign and a seal. As a sign, it is an emblem of the washing of regeneration, or the baptism of the Holy Ghost. It therefore signifies the same as circumcision. Does it not also seal the same? Does it not assure those that receive it, that if their characters are conformed to its sacred import, their faith shall be imputed to them for righteousness, and they be interested in all the blessings of the covenant of grace? But if, when the ancient token of the covenant was abolished, an ordinance was established in the same church, and appended to the same covenant, of precisely the same import, how is it possible to resist the conclusion, that this latter is substituted for the former?

So the instructions of the Scriptures confirm this view of the subject. Circumcision and baptism are used synonymously. Paul says to the Philippians, "Beware of the concision, (those who attached great importance to circumcision, and would insist upon it in relation to Gentile converts,) for we are the circumcision who worship God in spirit." To the Colossians he says, "Ye are circumcised with the circumcision made without hands, in putting off the body of the sins of the flesh, by the circumcision of Christ. Buried with him in baptism." That is, ye are circumcised by having been baptized into Christ. Here the word circumcision is evidently used for baptism. So the church in all ages have understood the subject. Then, if baptism stands in the place of circumcision, it ought to be applied in the same extent; and unless we are somewhere prohibited, it should be applied to the children of believing parents, as it has been in all ages, and will be to the end, especially by the Jews when they shall be grafted into "their own good olive-tree; for then their children shall be as aforetime."

4. The instructions of Christ and his apostles, can be reconciled upon no other principle, than that baptism, the token of the covenant, was designed, under the Christian dispensation, to be applied to children, and by the apostles was applied to them.

Upon this subject Dr. Pond remarks, "In order to determine what we might, or might not expect of Christ and his apostles, it will be necessary that we keep in mind the established customs of the period in which they lived. In the Jewish church, children had always been connected with their parents. They were early given up to God, and received the seal of his everlasting covenant. Also the children of proselytes were connected in covenant, with their parents, and entitled to the initial rites of circumcision and baptism. What then might be expected of Christ and his apostles, on the supposition that they intended to put an end to this state of things? Not silence surely. Silence would have been a virtual approbation of it. The further connection of children with parents they would have constantly condemned. They would have lost no opportunity of insisting on the great change, in this respect, which had taken place under the new dispensation, and of pressing a conformity to it in the practice of Christians. Did they pursue such a course? Never in any instance." Nor have they made the remotest allusion to any such change. But what might they be expected to have done, had they intended that the covenant relation of children should continue as it had been for two thousand years? Not indeed that it should be enjoined by any new precept. It was already enjoined by the very terms of the covenant; and unless expressly prohibited, would, of course, continue. It might be expected that Christ should approve the conduct of parents that brought babes to him for his blessing; that the apostles should baptize households, and speak of household baptism in the very manner in which they have done, as a consequence of the belief of the head.

No reader of the Bible need be informed that the terms house and household are used in the Scriptures in the same sense as we use family. Christ said to Zaccheus, "This day is salvation come to this house, forasmuch as he also is a son of Abraham;" that is, is a spiritual child of Abraham by faith. And in consequence of his faith, salvation had come to his family. The family seem to have been included in the blessing of the covenant, on account of the faith of the head. "Parents brought young children" (babes) "to Christ, ihat he should lay his hands on them and bless them, and his disciples rebuked them that brought them. But when Jesus saw it, he was much displeased, and said unto them, Suffer little children to come unto me, and forbid them not; for of such is the kingdom of heaven." These little children (babes) needed, and they were capable of receiving, and did receive the blessing of Christ. Christ required his disciples to permit little children to come unto him, and to forbid them not; for of such is the kingdom of heaven. The privileges and blessings of the kingdom belonged to them, and they were members of the kingdom. Here is instruction, put on record, for the direction of his servants in the ministry. Aware of the circumstances of the present period, in which many would rebuke parents that should bring their children publicly to him in an ordinance of his religion; Christ says, "Suffer little children to come unto me, and forbid them not;" because they are members of the kingdom of heaven on earth, as the phrase usually means. Ifv the passage be said to mean that adults, who are like little children, are of the kingdom of heaven; then, if they that are only like little children are fit for the kingdom of heaven, much more they, to whom they are like. Christians are fitted for the kingdom of heaven, because they are like Christ. If it be said that the kingdom of heaven means the kingdom of glory, and that little children are fit for this, then much more for the kingdom of heaven on earth. If it be said that Christ meant by his language, only that parents should bring their children to him in the arms of faith and prayer, then what is the use of the prohibition in the case? for who could forbid or prevent their doing it? And Christ would not enjoin it upon his disciples not to forbid, that is, to prevent parents doing that which they had no power to prevent. As soon might he have been expected to require his disciples not to forbid the winds to blow, or the sun to shine; for what man can control the immortal Spirit in its acts of faith and prayer; and most certainly Christ would not have the folly to require his disciples not to forbid little ones coming to him at death, in the kingdom of his glory. Then it can have reference only to the kingdom of heaven on earth—and of this kingdom only, can they be prevented from becoming members; here only in the ordinance of baptism, can his disciples forbid, that is, prevent their coming to Christ. Here then they are required not to forbid their coming.

In this place let us contemplate the expressions of the text in reference to this part of the subject. It is to be borne in mind that the instruction contained in the command was given to the Jews, who had always been in the habit of considering children as sustaining a covenant relation to God in connection with their parents: that upon them they had from the beginning been accustomed to put the token of the covenant of God—the seal of the righteousness of faith: that their prophet Isaiah says of the Gentiles, "They are the seed of the blessed, and their offspring with them:" and that Christ had given them no instructions, so far as we know, which would imply that the seal of the righteousness of faith was not still to be applied to children; but on the contrary, had expressly enjoined it upon them not to forbid little children to come unto him—and then the phraseology of the commission; "Go teach all nations, (disciple all nations,) baptizing them," etc. How would they necessarily understand this commission? And what is universally understood by the word nations? It will now be seen how Peter understood this commission, by the first sermon he ever preached after it was given. He evidently understood it as including children as well as parents. He said to the Jews, "The promise is unto you. and to your children." And does not the word nations, include children equally as their parents, little ones as well as adults? Are they not always included in the estimate of a nation? Now it cannot be shown that Christ did not include them, and require his disciples to baptize them, till it can be shown that the word nations does not include children. "Wetsein," says Dr. Pond, "makes three classes of disciples, those having been taught, those being taught, and those to be taught." Timothy is said to have been a disciple (*apo brephous*) from infancy. Justin Martyr, who wrote about forty years after the time of the apostles, says, "Several persons among us, of sixty or seventy years old, of both sexes, who were discipled to Christ (or made disciples) in or from their childhood, do continue uncorrupted."[16] Upon which Wall remarks, "St. Justin's word *ematheteuthesan*, were discipled or made disciples, is the very same word that had been used by St. Matthew, in expressing our Saviour's command, (*matheteusate*,) disciple or make disciples of all nations." According to Justin, those persons whom he mentions, then sixty or seventy years old, were made disciples from their childhood, that is, in the days of the apostles. The disciples could have understood their commission in no other light, than in accordance with the universal practice of the Jews, to make disciples of all nations, and to baptize, or place the token of the covenant upon believing parents and their children.

What was the practice of the apostles? It is granted that but little is said about baptism in the history of the acts of the apostles; but that little strongly favors the idea of infant baptism. It is a remarkable fact, that of the cases of baptism mentioned, so large a proportion, one-third or one-quarter of the whole, should be household baptisms. Paul baptized the household of Stephanas, the household of Lydia, and that of the jailer. Concerning the household of Stephanas, none of the circumstances are given; but it was household baptism. Now it is a matter of fact that Baptists never baptize households. In the case of Lydia and her household, the very face of the account shows conclusively, that Lydia was the only individual in her family that believed. "A certain woman named Lydia....heard us; whose heart the Lord opened, that *she* attended unto the things which were spoken of Paul. And when she was baptized, and her household, *she* besought us, saying, If ye have judged *me* to be faithful to the Lord, come into my house and abide there." In the case of the jailer, after Paul and Silas had preached the gospel to him and his family, "he (i. e. the jailer) took them the same hour of the night, and washed their stripes; and was baptized, he and *all his*, straightway. And when he had brought them into his house, he sat meat before them, and rejoiced, believing in God with all his house." In regard to the household of Lydia, the account furnishes no evidence whatever that any other member than herself believed, but on the contrary, that she, and she only believed; nor is there any incident mentioned that necessarily supposes that any of her family believed, or that even alludes to any thing of the kind. It is very strange that if any of the family of Lydia were believers, she should not have used language in her conversation with Paul that would have implied it. The historian speaks of Lydia, and of her only, as believing. *She* speaks of herself as the only believer in her house. The Lord opened her heart; *she* attended to the things spoken of Paul; *she* besought us, saying, If ye have judged *me* faithful; and when *she* believed, *she* was baptized, and her household. It is said, that we do not know that there were any little children in her family; nor, on the other hand, do we know that there were not. It is not of consequence to our position whether they were little children or not—they were under the government and instruction of Lydia; constituted her household, and were all baptized on her profession of faith. How do the Baptists prove that the members of her household were believers? Why, by showing that they were baptized, and by their baptism prove their faith. The very question at issue is taken for granted. It should be proved by them that her household believed, then they will establish their position so far as this case is concerned. It is assumed that the household of Lydia were believers, because, when Paul and Silas were released from prison, "they entered into the house of Lydia, and when they had seen the brethren, they comforted them and departed." Now by assuming without the slightest proof that the brethren here mentioned were the household of Lydia, they make true the former assumption that her household were all believers, and therefore supposed to be such before they were baptized. Even if it be admitted that her household were at this time believers, (of which there is no evidence,) how does it follow that they were believers when they were baptized? There was sufficient time, if they were capable of faith, for their conversion during the "many days" that Paul and Silas continued in that city. The supposition, however, directly contradicts the narrative of the sacred historian, i. e. the supposition which makes Lydia's household to have believed at the time she did. It was Lydia that heard Paul and Silas,—Lydia's heart that was opened. She attended to the things spoken; and when she was baptized and her household, she said, "If ye have judged me faithful," not my household. As to the assumption that the brethren whom Paul and Silas saw at Lydia's house and comforted, were the household of Lydia, it is without the shadow of foundation. It was evidently the church which they established at Philippi—the converts that were made to the gospel during the "many days" the apostles continued in that city. They would mutually desire to see each other. The converts, to be instructed and comforted by their teachers; and the teachers, to see and comfort those over whose conversion they had recently rejoiced, and to bid each other farewell before they separated. These converts were evidently scattered over the city. After Paul and Silas entered into the house of Lydia, they there tarried till the brethren could be collected. The narrative implies as much as this. "They entered into Lydia's house, and *when* they had seen the brethren," that is, when they had tarried in the house a sufficient time for the brethren to assemble, &c. Had Lydia's household constituted "the brethren," it should have been written, they entered into Lydia's house, saw the brethren, etc. The historian says, "They entered into Lydia's house, and *when* they *had* seen the brethren," implying that the time of their stay at Lydia's house was protracted for an opportunity of seeing the brethren. Concerning the jailer and his family, our opponents say, that the language, "He rejoiced, believing in God with all his house," implies that all his family believed. That a mere reader of English should be led to such a view of the subject, would not be very strange; but for one that can read the Greek Testament, to assert that the account says they all believed, is still more strange. Literally it is, He (*egalliasato*) rejoiced (*panoiki*) domestically, or in the midst of all his family, (*panoiki* being an adverb qualifying *egalliasato*,) (*pepisteukos*, perfect participle in the singular number,) he having believed (*to Theo*) in God. I say, then, it will be perfectly manifest to every one that candidly examines the subject in the original, that the account gives no intimation of any other believer in this family but the jailer. He (*pepisteukos*) having believed, "was baptized, and all his straightway;" they, that is, "all his" were baptized because they were his—because they belonged to a believing, covenanting head of a family. These two instances abundantly confirm the doctrine of household baptism in the sense in which we understand and use the term household baptism, according to which the household is baptized on account of the faith of the head.[17]

In 1 Cor. vii., is a passage of which they that deny infant baptism have not given even a plausible exposition; and which seems unintelligible, except upon the admission of the covenant relation of children, on account of the faith of the parent. "The unbelieving husband is sanctified by the wife, and the unbelieving wife is sanctified by the husband; else were your children unclean, but now are they holy." Our opponents say, in their exposition of the passage, that the faith of one of the parents rendered their marriage lawful, or that the unbelief of one did not render the marriage unlawful, so that their children were holy, that is, legitimate; otherwise, that is, if they had both been unbelievers, then were their children unholy, that is, illegitimate. This exposition is not even plausible. Or if "otherwise" may imply, that if it were not that the unbelieving parent were sanctified by the believing parent, then were the marriage unlawful, and the children illegitimate, it helps the matter but little: for even then an entirely unauthorized meaning is attached to the word holy —a meaning in which it is never used in the Bible. Holy, universally means, either that which is spiritually pure, or that which is relatively so. That which is sanctified, is either that which is holy in itself, or that which may be, or is devoted to God. In this latter sense, whatever is appropriated to the service of God, is said to be holy. The children of believing parents are relatively holy, as a consequence of their intimate connection with believing parents; so that it was proper to devote them to God in the ordinance of baptism. And the unbelieving partner was also relatively sanctified by the connection with a believer. The question whether the believer was to separate from the unbelieving partner, did not touch the legitimacy of their marriage, nor of their children. If we suppose this to be the case, the cause of the legitimacy of the children being the influence of the believer upon the unbeliever,—take away the cause, and the effect will, of course, cease; that is, take away the influence of the believing parent, let them both be in a state of unbelief, and their children will be illegitimate. An exposition that leads to such conclusions, is not even plausible.

Might it not have been a question with the Corinthians whether the children of parents, when only one was a believer, were in covenant relation, as were the children whom they had been accustomed to see baptized, both of whose parents were believers? Now might not this have been questioned,—and the question raised whether such believing parent ought not to separate from the unbelieving? Paul decided that no such separation was necessary; but that such was the influence of the believer upon the unbeliever, that their children were "holy." And being holy, it was proper that they should be consecrated to God in the ordinance of baptism. This is manifestly the plain exposition of the passage. In this general view agree all the commentators and critics, Baptists excepted. Who can believe that Paul ever taught the Corinthians that the faith of one of the parents made the marriage legal, and the children legitimate; when, if both the parents had been unbelievers, their marriage had been illegal, and their children illegitimate? Would such an interpretation ever have been conceived, had it not been for the necessity of getting rid of the subject of infant baptism? The passage, then, affords a strong evidence in favor of infant baptism. And if the children of parents, only one of whom is a believer, are holy, then much more, when both parents are believers.

5. I adduce in favor of the covenant relation of children with their parents, and consequently of infant baptism, an argument drawn from the providential government of God.

Something may be learned in regard to this subject from the providential government of God. It is objected to including children or infants in the covenant, that they are incapable of faith or holy exercises. So on the other hand it might be objected to their being included in the judgments of God, because they are incapable of any overt acts of wickedness, whatever may be said concerning their depraved nature. But what has been the course of Providence in relation to parents and their children? Have they not, even infants, always been connected with their parents both in the blessings and judgments of heaven? This, at least, has generally been the case. See the old world, when all the little ones were overwhelmed in the flood with their guilty parents; not because they had committed any overt acts of wickedness, but because they belonged to wicked parents. So also in the judgment upon Sodom—and all those cities that were overwhelmed with ruin—in which their little ones also perished. So on the other hand God has included the children in blessings bestowed upon pious parents, not because the children were capable of holy exercises, but because they belonged to pious parents, they were considered and treated as a part of themselves; as in the case of Noah and his family. God saved Noah because he was a righteous man, and all his children, his sons, and his sons' wives, and their children, if they had any, because they belonged to righteous Noah; when one of them, at least, was manifestly wicked. Also in the salvation of Lot from the destruction of Sodom, the angels said to him, "Hast thou here any besides? son-in-law, and thy sons, and thy daughters, and whatsoever thou hast in the city, bring them out of this place." Why? Because they belonged to Lot. But some of them were so hardened in wickedness that they would not even hearken to Lot.

In all the covenants which God has made with man, he has uniformly connected the children with the parents. This is true in regard to the covenants made with Adam, Noah, and with Abraham. In all cases God included the offspring with the parents. Adam violated the law of God in that covenant of works established with him, and all his posterity are involved in the consequences. Abraham believed God, and circumcision was placed upon him, as the seal of the righteousness of his faith, and also upon his household, and especially upon his son Isaac and his seed, as a part of himself. It is then according to the whole plan of the moral government of God, as unfolded in his acts, to include the children with the parents. Analogy would lead us to conclude that they would be included in the covenant of grace. And on this principle we understand this covenant as originally established with Abraham, and confirmed with the Christian church, and so they are included in the blessings of the gospel of the grace of God, unless we have something to the contrary in the positive instructions of the word of God. But there is nothing against, and much in favor of this conclusion; therefore we consider it to be according to the mind of the Lord Jesus, that little children should be brought to him in the ordinance of baptism.

II. *I adduce the testimony of ecclesiastical history in favor of infant baptism.*

Were history entirely silent upon the subject, still infant baptism would be established upon an immovable basis, by the evidence in its favor in the Scriptures. But the view which has now been taken of the subject, is abundantly confirmed by the history of the church.

In regard to this subject, Dr. Miller remarks,—

"I can assure you, my friends, with the utmost candor and confidence, after much careful inquiry on the subject, that, for more than fifteen hundred years after the birth of Christ, there was not a single society of professing Christians on earth, who opposed infant baptism on any

thing like the grounds which distinguish our modern
Baptist brethren. It is an undoubted fact, that the people
known in ecclesiastical history under the name of the
Anabaptists, who arose in Germany in 1522, were the
very first body of people, in the whole Christian world,
who rejected the baptism of infants, on the principles now
adopted by the Antipaedobaptist body.

"Tertullian, about two hundred years after the birth of
Christ, is the first man of whom we read in ecclesiastical
history, as speaking a word against infant baptism; and
he, while he recognizes the existence and prevalence of
the practice, and expressly recommends that infants be
baptized, if they are not likely to survive the period of
infancy; yet advises that, where there is a prospect of
their living, baptism be delayed until a late period of
life. But what was the reason of this advice? The moment
we look at the reason, we see that it avails nothing to
the cause in support of which it is sometimes produced.
Tertullian adopted the superstitious idea, that baptism was
accompanied with the remission of all past sins; and that
sins committed after baptism were peculiarly dangerous.
He therefore advised, that not merely infants, but young
men and young women, and even young widows and
widowers should postpone their baptism until the period
of youthful appetite and passion should have passed. In
short, he advised that, in all cases in which death was
not likely to intervene, baptism be postponed, until the
subjects of it should have arrived at a period of life, when
they would be no longer in danger of being led astray by
youthful lusts. And thus, for more than a century after the
age of Tertullian, we find some of the most conspicuous
converts to the Christian faith, postponing baptism till the
close of life. Constantine the Great, we are told, though
a professing Christian for many years before, was not

baptized till after the commencement of his last illness. The same fact is recorded of a number of other distinguished converts to Christianity about and after that time. But, surely, advice and facts of this kind make nothing in favor of the system of our Baptist brethren. Indeed, taken altogether, their historical bearing is strongly in favor of our system.

"The next persons that we hear of as calling in question the propriety of infant baptism, were the small body of people in France, about twelve hundred years after Christ, who followed a certain Peter de Bruis, and formed an inconsiderable section of the people known in ecclesiastical history under the general name of the Waldenses. This body maintained that infants ought not to be baptized, because they were incapable of salvation. They taught that none could be saved but those who wrought out their salvation by a long course of self-denial and labor. And as infants were incapable of thus c working out their own salvation,' they held that making them the subjects of a sacramental seal was an absurdity." This sect soon came to nought.

"We hear no more of any society or organized body of those who opposed infant baptism, until the sixteenth century, when they arose, as before stated, in Germany, and for the first time broached the doctrine of our modern Baptist brethren. As far as I have been able to discover, they were absolutely unknown in the whole Christian world, before that time.

"It is not only certain, that we hear of no society of Antipaedobaptists resembling our present Baptist brethren, for more than fifteen hundred years after Christ, but there is positive, direct proof that, during the whole of that time, infant baptism was the general and unopposed practice of the Christian church, with those exceptions now mentioned."

It will only be necessary to adduce testimony to show that infant baptism was the general practice of the church during the three or four first centuries; for after this, learned Baptists admit that infant baptism was the universal practice of the church.

Dr. Gill, one of the most learned opposers of infant baptism, admits, that infant baptism was the universal practice of the church from the third century to the eleventh, and not a single word was said against it.

Mr. Gales, an eminent Baptist writer, as quoted by Dr. Pond, says,—

"I will grant it is probable, that what all or most of the churches practiced immediately after the apostles' times, had been appointed or practiced by the apostles themselves; for it is hardly to be imagined that any considerable body of these ancient Christians, and much less that the whole, should so soon deviate from the customs and injunctions of their venerable founders, whose authority they held sacred. New opinions or practices, are usually introduced by degrees, and not without opposition. Therefore, in regard to baptism, a thing of such universal concern and daily practice, I allow it to be very probable that the primitive churches kept to the apostolic pattern."

Dr. Dwight says, (referring to Wall),—

"A person who employed himself extensively in examining this subject, gives the following as the result of his inquiries.

"First: During the first four hundred years from the formation of the Christian church, Tertullian only urged the delay of baptism to infants, and that only in some cases, and Gregory only delayed it perhaps, to his own children. But neither any society of men, nor any individual, denied the lawfulness of baptizing infants.

"Secondly: In the next seven hundred years, there was not a society, nor an individual, who even pleaded for this delay; much less any who denied the right, or the duty, of infant baptism.

"Thirdly: In the year 1120, one sect of the Waldenses declared against the baptism of infants; because they supposed them incapable of salvation. But the main body of that people rejected the opinion as heretical; and the sect which held it, soon came to nothing.

"Fourthly: The next appearance of this opinion was in 1522." "Hermas," (quoted from Dr. Pond,) "mentioned by Paul, and who is supposed to have written before John wrote his gospel, says, 'All infants are in honor with the Lord, and are esteemed first of all.'"

Justin Martyr, who wrote about forty years after the apostolic age, says, "Several persons among us of sixty or seventy years old, of both sexes, were discipled (or made disciples) to Christ (*ex paidon*) from their childhood."[18] They could be made disciples from their infancy only by baptism, and that many years before the death of the apostle John.

Irenaeus, who was born not far from the time of the death of the apostle John, and who wrote about sixty-seven years after the apostolic age, says, "Christ came to save all persons by himself: All, I mean, who, by him, are baptized, infants and little ones, and children, and youths, and elder persons."[19]

Says Wall, "Origen, Ambrose, and Austin, do, each of them, expressly affirm, that baptizing infants was ordered by the apostles and practiced in their time."[20]

Tertullian admitted the universal practice of infant baptism in the churches, yet advised its delay, as before shown, and for the causes specified. In the very act of advising its delay, he admitted it to be the common practice. And, says Prof. Stuart, "It is certain that infant baptism was in general practice in Tertullian's day, the first century after the apostles."

Origen, who was born about eighty-five years after the apostles, gives clear and definite testimony in relation to the practice of infant baptism in his day. He says, "Infants are baptized for the forgiveness of sins. Of what sins? or when have they sinned? or how can any reason of the laver in their case hold good, but according to that sense that we mentioned even now; none is free from pollution, though his life be but the length of one day upon the earth? And it is for this reason, because, by the sacrament of baptism the pollution of our birth is taken away, that infants are baptized. For this, also, it was, that the church had from the apostles a tradition, or order, to give baptism even to infants."[21] This leaves us no ground to question what was the practice of the church in the first and second centuries after the apostles: that infant baptism was universally practiced, and the churches understood that such were the instructions of the apostles. And there is no possibility that the whole church should thus early have fallen into the practice of infant baptism, had it been an innovation upon the practice of the apostles, and contrary to their instructions.

Cyprian, an eminently godly man, and bishop of Carthage, flourished about the middle of the second century. In his day, about one hundred and fifty years after the apostles, a council of sixty-six bishops or ministers, was assembled at Carthage to consider a variety of matters relative to the church. Among other subjects, that of infant baptism was taken into consideration, as presented to them by one Fidus. The question was not, whether it was proper and apostolical to baptize infants. No one doubted it. And it seems to have been the universally received opinion of the church, that baptism had taken the place of circumcision, and was applied like that, to the offspring as well as the adult. Fidus had presented to this council of sixty-six ministers the question, whether it were lawful to administer baptism to an infant before it was eight days old. The answer of the council to this question is as follows:

"Cyprian, and the rest of the bishops who were present at the council, sixty-six in number, to Fidus our brother, greeting: As to the case of infants, whereas you judge that they must not be baptized within two or three days after they are born, and that the rule of circumcision is to be observed, so that none should be baptized and sanctified until the eighth day after he is born, we were all in our assembly of the contrary opinion. For, as for what you thought fitting to be done, there was not one that was of your mind, but all of us, on the contrary, judged that the grace and mercy of God is to be denied to no person that is born.... This, therefore, dear brother, was our opinion in the assembly: that it is not for us to hinder any person from baptism and the grace of God, who is merciful, and kind, and affectionate to all. Which rule, as it holds for all, so we think it more especially in reference to infants and persons newly born."[22] Here, then, we have an assembly of sixty-six ministers, convened from various parts of the Christian church, one hundred and fifty years after the apostles, called upon to decide the question whether baptism were lawfully administered, in case of infants, before the eighth day after birth. Concerning the whole subject of infant baptism, this assembly was unanimous. And among so many, was there none that knew that infant baptism was an innovation upon the practice of the apostles? Or, at least, if it had been, was there none that had ever heard of it? And was there none, that had a sufficiency of apostolical integrity and boldness to raise his voice against this corruption? These were not men that were afraid to stand up against public opinion, and evea to meet persecution in defence of the truth. Had infant baptism been an innovation upon the practice of the apostles, there is a moral certainty that they must have known it; they must have known when, and where such an error first began. As Mr. Gales says, there must have been controversy upon the subject; and the writings upon the subject must have been in their possession. And there is a moral certainty too, that had infant baptism been contrary to the instructions of Christ, and the practice of the apostles, the Lord would have taken care that his doctrine should somewhere have been preserved pure in the church; and it is also certain that the church could not thus early have fallen into the practice of infant baptism, had it not been the practice of the apostles and their immediate successors. And from the fact that there was no one to utter a word against the practice, it is evident that it had always been the custom of the churches, and was practiced by the apostles. It might with as much plausibility be pretended, that we do not now know what were the views and practice of the Pilgrims that landed on Plymouth rock, upon this subject, as that the ministers in the days of Cyprian did not for certainty know what were the views and practice of the apostles.

In the apostolical constitutions ascribed to Clement of Rome, it is written, "Baptize your infants, and bring them up in the nurture and admonition of the Lord."[23]

In a work entitled Questions and Answers to the Orthodox, an ancient work, which some have ascribed to Justin Martyr, who lived about forty years after the apostles, it is written, "This will be the difference between those that have been baptized, and those that have not: that the baptized will be made partakers of the blessings of baptism; and the unbaptized, not. And these blessings of baptism are vouchsafed to them for the sake of the faith of those that bring them to baptism."[24]

I pass by the testimony of many of the early fathers upon the subject of infant baptism, and add only that of Augustine and Pelagius. I give their testimony principally as it is given by Dr. Miller, in his Sermons on Baptism. Augustine flourished about 290 or 300 years after the apostles; and was one of the most pious, learned and venerable fathers of the Christian church. Pelagius, the learned heretic, lived at the same time, and had travelled through France, Italy, Africa Proper to Jerusalem. Pelagius denied original sin; and maintained the purity of infants. Augustine opposing him, asks, "Why are infants baptized for the remission of sins, if they have no sin?"—intimating that Pelagius, to be consistent, must deny the propriety of infant baptism. The reply of Pelagius is striking and unequivocal, "Baptism," says he, "ought to be administered to infants, with the same sacramental words which are used in the case of adult persons. Men slander me as if I denied the sacrament of baptism to infants. I never heard of any, not even the most impious heretic, who denied baptism to infants; for who can be so impious as to hinder infants from being baptized, and born again in Christ, and so make them miss of salvation?" Again, Augustine remarks, "Since they grant that infants must be baptized, as not being able to resist the authority of the whole church, which was doubtless delivered by our Lord and his apostles, they must consequently grant that they stand in need of the benefit of the Mediator; that being offered by the sacrament, and by the charity of the faithful, and so being incorporated into Christ's body, they may be reconciled to God." Again, speaking of certain heretics at Carthage, he says, "They, minding the Scriptures, and the authority of the whole church, and the form of the sacrament itself, see well that baptism in infants is for the remission of sins." In another case he says, "Which the whole body of the church holds in the case of little infants baptized; who certainly cannot believe with the heart unto righteousness, or confess with the mouth unto salvation; nay, by their crying and noise while the sacrament is administering, they disturb the holy mysteries: and yet no Christian man will say that they are baptized to no purpose." Again Augustine says, "The custom of our mother, the church, in baptizing infants, must not be disregarded, nor accounted needless, nor believed to be any thing else than an ordinance delivered to us from the apostles." Concerning these facts, Dr. Miller remarks, "Here then were two men, undoubtedly among the most learned then in the world,... who never saw or heard of any one who called himself a Christian, not even the most impious heretic; no, nor any writer who claimed to believe in the Scriptures, who denied the baptism of infants. Can the most incredulous reader, who is not fast bound in the fetters of invincible prejudice, hesitate to admit, *first*, that these men verily believed that infant baptism had been the universal practice of the church from the days of the apostles? and *secondly*, that situated and informed as they were, it was impossible that they should be mistaken?" Could such a great change as the unauthorized introduction of infant baptism have been brought about in the church, and these men not have known it? Impossible. Much more testimony of the same character might be added from those who lived in the first centuries of the Christian church, but the foregoing is sufficient; and they that will not be convinced by that now adduced, would not, by the addition of much more to the same point. The testimony from the early history of the church, is entirely conclusive and irresistible, that infant baptism was the universal practice of the church from the days of the apostles; and, of course, must have been practiced by the apostles.

When the inquiry has been made as to where the Baptist church was to be found prior to the time when the Anabaptists arose in 1522, it is immediately answered that the Waldenses were Baptists; but they certainly are not Baptists now; and for generations, yea for centuries past have not been: and they probably know as well as any, what their fathers were. They say, "We present our children in baptism," "we bring our children to be baptized." And said the Rev. Mr. Burt, the moderator of their synod, to Rev. Mr. Dwight, then of Boston, a few years ago, "We have always baptized our infants, and have always baptized them by affusion."

Upon this subject Dr. Miller remarks,—

"It is here worthy of particular notice, that those pious and far-famed witnesses for the truth, commonly known by the name of the Waldenses, did undoubtedly hold to the doctrine of infant baptism, and practice accordingly. In their Confessions of Faith, and other writings, drawn up between the twelfth and sixteenth centuries, and in which they represent their creeds and usages as handed down from father to son for several hundred years before the reformation, they speak on the subject before us, so frequently and explicitly, as to preclude all doubt in regard to the fact alleged. The following specimen of their language will satisfy every reasonable inquirer. 'Baptism,' say they, is administered in a full congregation of the faithful, to the end that he that is received into the church, may be reputed and held of all as a Christian brother; and that all the congregation may pray for him, that he may be a Christian in heart, as he is outwardly esteemed to be a Christian. And for this cause it is that we present our children in baptism, which ought to be done by those to whom the children are most nearly related, as their parents, or those to whom God has given this charity.'

"Understanding that their Popish neighbors charged them with denying the baptism of infants, they acquit themselves of this imputation as follows. 'Neither is the time or place appointed for those who are to be baptized. But charity, and the edification of the church and congregation, ought to be the rule in this matter. Yet notwithstanding, we bring our children to be baptized; which they ought to do to whom they are most nearly related, such as parents, or those whom God hath inspired with such a charity.'"

"True it is," adds the historian,—

"that being for some hundreds of years constrained to suffer their children to be baptized by the Romish priests, they deferred the performance of it as long as possible, because they detested the human inventions annexed to that holy sacrament, which they looked upon as so many pollutions of it. On account of which delay, the priests have charged them with that reproach."

It being so plainly a fact, established by their own unequivocal and repeated testimony, that the great body of the Waldenses were Paedobaptists, on what ground is it that our Baptist brethren assert, and that some have been found to credit the assertion, that those venerable witnesses of the truth rejected the baptism of infants? The answer is plain. A small sect of people going under the general name of Waldenses, the followers of Peter de Bruis, and called Petrobrusians, denied baptism to infants, as before stated, and for the reason, as they said, that they were incapable of salvation. This sect, which arose in the eleventh century, soon came to nought; while the great body of the Waldenses always practiced infant baptism: of this, evidence is clear and full. Another fact which establishes the views and practice of the Waldenses, is that they readily united with the reformed churches of Geneva and Germany, and sought from them pastors for their own churches, which they would not have done had they not been Paedobaptists; and such they continue to be at the present day.

The amount of historical evidence against infant baptism, during the first fifteen hundred years of the Christian church, is, First, That in about a hundred years after the apostles, one Tertullian was found to advise the delay of baptism, not only in the case of infants, but also in adults, because he believed that baptism washed away all former sins,—and that sins committed after baptism were peculiarly heinous. Secondly, In the eleventh century, a small sect, the Petrobrusians, which soon came to nought, denied baptism to infants, because they believed them incapable of salvation. And the evidence is clear, that all the rest of the Christian church, during all this period, practised infant baptism. It is granted by learned Baptists, that from the fourth to the eleventh century, no one questioned the right of infant baptism. And the evidence is clear, that till Tertullian advised the delay of baptism, no one questioned its propriety; and from the eleventh century to the fifteenth, none questioned the propriety of infant baptism but the Petrobrusians, because, as they said, infants could not be saved. Then it follows conclusively, that there was no Baptist church in the world, on present Baptist principles, till it existed among the Anabaptists in 1522. Baptist principles being true, then it follows that for near fifteen hundred years God had no church in the world; and for seven hundred years, according to the admission of the Baptists, that is, from the fourth to the eleventh century, during which period they admit that not a word was said against infant baptism, there could have been no true church. And it is difficult to conceive how a true or Baptist church could come into existence, without a new revelation, and a new commission to some one to baptize. Baptism, according to their view, to be valid, must be administered by immersion to a believer, and the administrator be a person immersed subsequent to his faith. Baptists admit that for seven hundred years infant baptism was universally practised in the church. How then, according to their views, could a regular Baptist church be brought into existence, as there was no one duly authorized to administer baptism, unless by a new commission from the Lord—except they did, as in the case of Roger Williams and company, appoint a committee to baptize one, and then he baptize the rest? But would it be valid baptism?

It is then upon Baptist principles true, that from near the time of the apostles till the sixteenth century, there was no true church in the world—and, indeed, according to their principles, there can be no genuine Baptist church in the world even now, for every Baptist church must have arisen as did the Baptist church in this country, in the case of Roger Williams, who was baptized by a committee appointed for that purpose, and then the committee and others were baptized by Williams. But was this, according to Baptist views, valid? and was the church made up of persons thus baptized, a genuine church? They will not pretend that baptism is valid when administered by an unauthorized person; or that those baptisms administered by persons baptized in infancy, are valid. Then how long must be the succession of invalid baptisms, before the baptism becomes valid, and the church a true church? Indeed, it is manifestly impossible for Baptists to show, that, according to their own principles, they have any true church in the world —for trace their baptism back as they will, they will come to the period when there was no valid baptism—none duly authorized (that is, according to their principles) to administer it,—and no succession, or repetition of invalid baptisms can render it valid and good. Views that lead to such conclusions and consequences, must manifestly be erroneous.

Lastly, a brief notice of some of the objections to infant baptism, will conclude this discourse.

It is objected to infant baptism, that baptism is a positive institution, and that "according to the law of positive institutions," there must be an explicit command to authorize it; that is, that there must be found in the New Testament a requisition in so many words, to baptize infants. We say, that from the very nature of the case, this is not necessary. As infants were originally included in the covenant, and to them was applied the token of the covenant, and no alteration having been made in the covenant, only a change in the token, or seal, it is of course to be applied to the same subjects, as under the Jewish dispensation, unless we have some directions to the contrary; but as there are none, baptism, being the token of the covenant under the Christian dispensation, is to be applied to believers, or

"the blessed of the Lord, and their offspring with them."
Still the Baptist says, that for positive institutions, we must
have positive precepts,—and asks triumphantly, Where is it
written, in all the Bible, that infants must be baptized? But
why do they lay down a general principle, when they are
not willing to abide by it? They do not in some other cases
act upon the principle which they lay down. The Sabbath
is a positive institution, and there is no obligation to keep
holy one day in seven, except by the express injunction
of the Lord. Now, we observe the first day of the week as
the Christian Sabbath, but there is no precept in the Bible
requiring us to observe the first day of the week as the
Sabbath. What authority have they for keeping the first day
of the week as the Sabbath? Certainly they have no positive
precept for it. The Lord's supper also is a positive institution,
not less so than baptism; and according to their principle,
they ought to have explicit instructions for all that they
do, in regard to this institution. There is no precept in the
Bible, which requires females to come to the communion
of the Lord's supper; nor is there, in the New Testament,
any example of their having come to this ordinance. To be
consistent with their principle, our Baptist brethren ought
to exclude females from the Lord's supper. Yet in view of the
reasonableness of the things themselves, and the practice of
the churches in the early ages, they are perfectly willing to
lay aside their principle in regard to positive institutions, and
are satisfied to keep the first day of the week as the Sabbath,
and to admit females to the Lord's supper. The objection,
therefore, is not to be urged by them; they themselves will
not abide by the principle; even their own objection has no
weight in their own minds.

Again, it is objected that infants are incapable of faith

and repentance, implied in baptism, and that these are required as prerequisites to this ordinance. True, in case of unbaptized adults they are; and by Paedobaptists evidence of faith and repentance is universally required prior to baptism. All those cases referred to, as proving that faith and repentance must be before baptism, are cases of adult persons, concerning which, all are agreed that there should be required evidence of faith and repentance before baptism. To assume that faith and repentance must precede baptism in all cases, is assuming the subject in debate. And because Peter said to the inquirers on the day of Pentecost, "Repent and be baptized every one of you," and Philip to the eunuch, upon his inquiry, What hindered him to be baptized? "If thou believest with all thine heart thou mayest," Dr. Chapin says, by baptizing before faith, that is, infants, we "reverse the order of God; and especially because it is written, 'He that believeth and is baptized shall be saved.'" So it may be answered that by insisting in all cases upon faith before baptism, we reverse the order of Christ, who says, "Except a man be born of water, and of the Spirit, he cannot enter into the kingdom of God." Now if the fact of faith in one case being mentioned before baptism, proves that in all cases faith must precede baptism; so, in the other case, water baptism, in the order of the words, standing before regeneration by the Spirit, proves, that in all cases baptism must precede regeneration. Hence, the mere order in which the things are mentioned in a sentence proves nothing, because it proves things directly contrary the one to the other. And that cause which needs to be supported by such kind of proof, stands very much in need of proof. It has already been proved that infants are scripturally subjects of the ordinance of baptism; and all those arguments and declarations which go to show that faith and repentance are required in case of adults, do not in any sense touch the question of infant baptism.

Again, it is objected that baptism is a token of the covenant of God, and that infants are incapable of entering into a covenant. It is, however, most certain that the little ones of Israel did enter into covenant with the Lord their God. "Ye stand this day all of you before the Lord your God; your captains of your tribes, your elders, and your officers, with all the men of Israel, your little ones, your wives, and thy stranger that is in thy camp, from the hewer of thy wood, unto the drawer of thy water; that thou shouldest enter into covenant with the Lord thy God, and into his oath, which the Lord thy God maketh with thee this day." Here it is manifest that the infant sustained a covenant relation to God equally with the parent. Infants are then capable of sustaining a covenant relation to God. Their parents acted for them in this transaction. That which they were capable of then, they are capable of now.

The objection here made against infant baptism, lies with all its force against infant circumcision. Baptism no more implies faith and a covenant, than did circumcision. So that condemning infant baptism, because infants are not capable of faith and entering into covenant, we condemn the judgment and acts of God. God judged infants capable of sustaining a covenant relation to himself, and had them brought before him, that, with their parents, they might enter into covenant with the Lord their God. In the same sense they are capable of entering into covenant with the Lord now.

Baptism implies a covenant transaction—so did circumcision. Baptism implies repentance and faith—so did circumcision. Abraham believed God, and it was counted to him for righteousness; and he received circumcision, a seal of the righteousness of faith which he had, being yet uncircumcised. And Abraham was required to place this token of the covenant and "seal of the righteousness of faith" upon his child eight days old. Now the same principles and spirit which, at the present time, are opposed to infant baptism, had they existed in the days of Abraham, would have said to Abraham—"From the nature of the case, it is wrong to circumcise the child; because circumcision implies a covenant transaction, and is a seal of the righteousness of faith, and this child only eight days old, is incapable of entering into covenant with God, incapable of faith, it is therefore improper to circumcise the child. Wait till the child shall by his own individual act avouch the Lord Jehovah to be his God, and believe in the promise of God concerning the Messiah, then circumcise him." But still the command of God was explicit that the token of his gracious covenant and the seal of the righteousness of faith should be placed upon the child when it was eight days old. This objection lies with equal force against infant circumcision, as against infant baptism, and so it stands against the judgment of God.

Again, it is said that it can do children no good to baptize them. So it might have been said with equal propriety that it could do the child no good to circumcise it. The child understood nothing about that covenant transaction of which circumcision was a token, and was incapable of the "righteousness of faith," of which it was the seal. The mere application of water in baptism does an adult no good. It is not designed to wash away the filth of the flesh; and it makes one neither holier nor wiser. But it is a token which God has appointed of his gracious covenant.

It is a symbol of important things, and calculated to impress upon the heart and conscience, the great truths and duties of the Christian religion. It is a sign and seal which God has appointed, and which he regards, remembering his holy covenant. God says, "As the soul of the father, so also the soul of the son is mine." And if God claims little children as his, and requires their believing parents to place upon them the token of his covenant, the seal of the righteousness of faith, connecting with this token, on condition of faithfulness in the parents, a promise that he will do for them all that is implied in this covenant transaction, then it may indirectly be of inestimable benefit to them. If it is calculated to impress upon the mind of the parent just views of the moral character of the child, its depraved nature, and of the necessity of its being born again by the renewing of the Holy Ghost, and of the heart being cleansed by the application of "the blood of sprinkling," and of his obligation to train it up for God, and to seek for it the blessings of divine grace, then it is calculated to do the child good; for whatever fixes these considerations more deeply in the mind of the parent, and excites to unceasing fidelity in the duties arising from the relation he sustains to his child as an immortal being, and a subject of the moral government of God, is of immense value to the child. God has made the moral character and eternal condition of children to depend, in no small measure, upon the faith and fidelity of parents. "Train up a child," says Solomon, "in the way he should go, and when he is old he will not depart from it." When parents are faithful, God pours out upon them his Spirit, and "his blessing upon their offspring."

Again, it is objected that what is implied in the ordinance of baptism, does not always take place in regard to those that are baptized in infancy. Nor is it true that what is implied in baptism always exists in those that are baptized in adult age, either before or after their baptism. Thousands have been baptized, even by immersion, in adult age, who had neither faith nor repentance. It is not true that what was implied in circumcision always took place in adult age. But was infant circumcision therefore useless and wrong? And is adult baptism wrong because many baptized, immersed even, have no repentance or faith, and afterwards apostatize? What argument, then, is it against infant baptism, that all baptized infants do not afterwards become truly pious? Is parental unfaithfulness an argument against the propriety and utility of infant baptism? There can be no doubt that the benefits implied in infant baptism would more generally be realized, if parents were more faithful in their covenant obligations. Indeed entire parental fidelity would in all cases secure the blessings of the covenant to children given to God in baptism. Parental unfaithfulness is itself made an objection to infant baptism, and baptism is deemed useless in regard to children. But this is making the abuse of a thing an argument against it, as though we should object to eating, because some persons are gluttonous. The same argument will lie against every part of the Christian religion; for what is there connected with this religion which has not been abused? We are constrained to acknowledge a great deficiency in regard to parental instruction, both by precept and example; and that parents but indifferently discharge the obligations to their children which they have consecrated to the service of the Lord, in the sacred ordinance of baptism. When Christians shall more conscientiously, faithfully, and perseveringly perform their covenant obligations to their baptized children, in restraining, governing and instructing them, then will they see more clearly, and experience more constantly the faithfulness of their covenant-keeping God; and the blessing of Abraham will come upon them and upon their seed; for, as Paul to the Galatians says, "They which are of faith, the same are the children of Abraham." "They which be of faith are blessed with faithful Abraham." Again, "If ye be Christ's, then are ye Abraham's seed, and heirs according to the promise." Once more, he says, "Now we, brethren, as Isaac was, are the children of promise." These declarations can mean nothing less, than that these Galatians, Gentile believers, were the children of that promise contained in the covenant made with Abraham, so they are "Abraham's seed," and "heirs according to the promise;" then with Abrahamic fidelity, all they that are the seed of Abraham by faith, will experience the blessing of Abraham, and command their household after them, for "they are the blessed of the Lord, and their offspring with them."

The more we examine this subject the more fully are we confirmed in our views of infant baptism, as being in perfect accordance with the entire economy of God's government of this world; and with all the covenants which God has made with man. And we are fully persuaded that it is in accordance with the mind and will of the Lord Jesus Christ, and the practice of the apostles; and we know it to have been the universal practice of the church in the first centuries, back to within forty years of the time of the apostles, when Justin Martyr wrote, as well as we know any historical fact. "It is certain," says Prof. Stuart, "that infant baptism was in general practice, the first century after the apostles." Dr. Woods, also, shows the same thing in his *Lectures on Infant Baptism.*

We esteem it a precious privilege, that we may dedicate our children to God in baptism. "Infant baptism," says Dr. Woods, "when apprehended correctly, must be agreeable to the best feelings of pious parents respecting their infant offspring." And according to their faithfulness, may they claim the fulfillment of the promise of God, that the blessing of Abraham should come upon them and their offspring; for according to the declaration of Peter, the promise is unto us and our children. We cannot, therefore, but consider those who reject infant baptism, in a great error; forbidding little children to be brought to Christ.

By rejecting infant baptism, they do that, which the most learned men, about three hundred years after the apostles, never knew, or heard of any man's doing that professed to be a Christian; no, not even the most impious heretic. They exclude from the covenant of God those whom he includes in it. It leads many lightly to esteem the instructions of the Old Testament, those Scriptures to which Christ and the apostles constantly referred their hearers. 'And it leads them also to neglect the moral and spiritual interests of their children; at least, those motives which arise from infant baptism, and they are many and strong, do not act upon them. Still we should exercise towards them that charity which suffereth long and is kind; and if the feeling is not returned, but on the contrary, bitterness and railing, still we should not be betrayed into the exercise of an unchristian spirit towards them. If they reject us from their communion, let us always endeavor to convince them of their wrong by our uniform kindness and charity; for "love worketh no ill to his neighbor." And while we cheerfully leave others to the exercise of their judgment and conscience, we claim the same right for ourselves, and shall believe that

Christ approves and requires household baptism, while his command remains in the Bible, "Go ye therefore and teach all nations, baptizing them in the name of the Father, and of the Son, and of the Holy Ghost."

CONCLUSION

DISCOURSES VII

"Let us hear the conclusion of the whole matter."
—Ecclesiastes xii. 13.

I HAVE, in several discourses, brought to view the often agitated question of baptism, both in regard to the mode and the subjects of this ordinance. There are still a few things which I wish to say, in connection with a recapitulation of the principal points, which I conceive to have been established upon this subject. In discussing this subject I have brought forward only a part of the evidence by which our views of it are sustained, yet enough to satisfy all candid and unbiased minds, that our views are abundantly sustained, both by Scripture and history.

It has been shown that neither Christ nor his apostles have said or done any thing in regard to the subject of baptism, which authorizes us to say that this or that mode exclusively is baptism; that is, we are not authorized to say that sprinkling only is baptism acceptable to the Lord Jesus

Christ; neither can we say this concerning immersion, or any other mode; that neither Christ nor his apostles have any where described a particular mode of baptism, which must be used to render baptism valid: therefore we conclude it is an error to state that immersion only is baptism; that there is no warrant for this either in the Bible or in history.

It has also been shown that *baptizo*, and its derivatives *baptisma* and *baptismos*, are not in any lexicons of the Greek language, limited to the meaning of immersion, and to immerse; but that, to wash, to tinge, to dye, to besprinkle are included in their meaning. It has been shown that both Mark and Luke use the word *baptizo* in reference to the application of water to the hands only, that is, in the daily washing of the hands, when they came from the market, before eating and at other times. And this washing of the hands was, in the estimation of Mark and Luke, baptism; and it seems to me, that they were right. And if they were right, then to be baptized does not require that the whole person should be plunged under water. It has also been shown that the apostle Paul includes in the meanings of *baptismos*, (baptism,) sprinkling; and that all those sprinklings practiced in the symbolical purifications of the Jews, were baptisms. Also, it has been shown, that, in the church immersion was never considered essential to baptism; that even Cyprian, one hundred and fifty years after tbe apostles, quoted from Ezekiel the passage, "Then will I sprinkle clean water upon you and ye shall be clean," in justification of baptism by sprinkling: that a variety of modes always were practiced in the church; and that immersion was never considered essential to baptism till the sixteenth century; therefore we conclude that immersion is not necessary to the validity of baptism.

It has been shown, that there is nothing in any of the circumstances mentioned, as attending the baptisms recorded in the New Testament, which makes it certain that immersion was the mode; indeed, there is nothing that renders it even probable; but on the contrary, such were the circumstances in numbers of cases, as rendered immersion impracticable, and make it morally certain that those baptisms were performed either by sprinkling or affusion.

It is also manifest that Christ Jesus does not regard the mode of baptism essential to its validity, from the fact, that he has greatly blessed churches, that have practiced sprinkling and affusion, with the effusions of the Holy Spirit, in genuine revivals of religion, that have resulted in the conversion and salvation of multitudes, and promoted extensively in the world piety and godliness; and that the Lord has inspired many of the members of these churches with a spirit of missions, that heavenly spirit of benevolence, which has gone forth for the moral renovation and redemption of the world. When the Lord has required his people to do any thing in a particular mode, he has always showed them the pattern, and required them to follow the pattern without deviation. Had Jesus Christ intended that all his church should have been baptized in a particular mode, he would have pointed out that mode so clearly, that all sincere inquirers after truth, could easily ascertain it, and without the danger of making a mistake. Had Christ designed that immersion should be exclusively the mode of baptism he would so clearly have pointed out that mode, that they, who, on account of the wishes of their friends and other circumstances, have strongly desired to find the principles of the Baptists in the Bible, would readily have discovered them. Yet there have been such, who, after much searching, have not been able to find these principles in the word of God. And some who imagine that they have found them, afterwards lose sight of them and are never able to discover them again.

It is, indeed, sometimes asked triumphantly, if the peculiar views of Baptists are erroneous, why they do not sometimes change their sentiments; supposing (what is by no means true) that such a change was never known. I am myself acquainted with several ministers who have left the Baptists. In a recent publication it is said, that in Germany, Baptists are becoming Paedobaptists by thousands. And hundreds of churches of that denomination have changed their views in regard to the mode of baptism; that is, have laid aside the practice of immersion, and baptize by affusion. And before I conclude, I will give some extracts from a recent publication of a neighboring clergyman, formerly a Baptist.

I have shown that sprinkling or affusion is a symbol of the inward cleansing of the heart by the Holy Spirit, and that this is indicative of the manner in which the Spirit is given; so that this mode of outward baptism represents the mode of the inward purification, when man is baptized by the Holy Spirit. And that at no time, since the world began, has Christ given to any church or individual, any mark of his displeasure, because there was not a sufficient quantity of water used in the administration of the ordinance of baptism. Whence the conclusion upon this subject is, First, that the meaning of the words rendered baptism and to baptize, is cleansing and to cleanse; and that baptism is an emblem of the inward cleansing of the heart by the effusions of the Holy Spirit; and that the mode of baptism most nearly resembling the Spirit's operations is a proper mode, and acceptable to Christ.

And therefore we conclude that that mode of administration which is convenient, decent, orderly and solemn, and indicative of the manner in which the Spirit is given; which may be performed at all times, and with perfect safety to persons in every condition in life, is agreeable to the will of Christ.

In the religious services of the Jews, most cf their symbolical cleansings or purifications were performed by sprinkling. "And the Lord spake unto Moses, saying, Take the Levites from among the children of Israel, and cleanse them. And thus shalt thou do unto them to cleanse them: sprinkle water of purifying upon them." In the case of cleansing from the plague of the leprosy; for his moral cleansing the leper was to be sprinkled seven times with the blood of the bird killed: and to cleanse the outward man from the filth of this disease, he was required to wash all his body; that is, to wash away the filth of the flesh. We are, then, satisfied that the mode of cleansing by sprinkling is one that was introduced into the church by the express command of God; was practiced in all ages of the church under the Jewish dispensation; was in practice when Christ came; when he gave his command to his disciples, and after his ascension; that this was the mode of moral purification symbolically, with water or blood, practiced at the temple at the time the apostles preached the gospel, till the temple was destroyed, and the daily sacrifice taken away. Wherefore, it would be perfectly natural that the apostles, who were Jews, as they must have understood baptism to be a symbolical cleansing, representing inward purification by the Holy Spirit, should practice that mode, to which they had long been accustomed, especially as they were never instructed to the contrary; and therefore we conclude that they who make immersion exclusively baptism, do so without any express warrant from Christ or his apostles, either by precept or example, by which Christ has signified his preference of that mode rather than any other. And in making immersion exclusively baptism, the Baptist violates his own principles. Baptism is a positive institution, and according to his principles, he should do nothing in regard to it, for which he has not a positive precept; but he has no positive precept pointing out immersion as the mode of baptism. He will doubtless answer that the command to baptize, is a positive precept to do it by immersion only, but he says this against a very great weight of evidence to the contrary. Even Mr. Carson, while he asserts that *baptizo* means only to immerse, acknowledges that he has all the Greek lexicographers against him. So that we conclude that he and his brethren must be wrong, and that the command to baptize, is not a command to perform baptism by immersion.

To constitute baptism good and valid, it must, says the Baptist, be performed by immersion, the administrator himself having been baptized by immersion, and so back by a succession of immersions to the days of the apostles to whom the command to baptize was given. We then conclude that, according to Baptist principles, there is no church in the United States, not even a regular Baptist church, formed according to their own principles; for the commencement of the Baptist church in this country, was in Roger Williams of Rhode Island. There, under the influence of Williams, a few persons assembled and formed the first Baptist church in this country. Now as none of these persons had been immersed, it is rather difficult to conceive how, according to Baptist principles, they could constitute themselves a regular Baptist church. How could they take a step towards it? No one was authorized, according to their view, to administer baptism by immersion. The method in which they proceeded was this. They appointed a committee, who immersed Roger Williams, then he immersed the rest. Williams himself afterwards concluded that they were all wrong, and that there could be no more a regular church in the world, until there should be a new revelation or commission from heaven, to organize the church anew. "Prof. Knowles, in his life of Roger Williams, intimates that the Roger Williams church is not the mother of all the close communion churches in this country, and thus he attempts to evade the above consequence. But we learn from Mosheim[25], that the first close communion church in England was formed in 1633, (that is, six years before the Roger Williams church,) and probably upon the same principles as that at Providence; so that it is immaterial whether this latter be the mother of all the close communion churches in this country or not. In either case it is true, that the opposers of infant baptism have no proof that their baptism is received from men who were themselves immersed."[26] This principle of exclusive immersion not only unchurches all those that do not hold to it, but even those that do.

Again, according to another principle of the Baptist denomination, we conclude, that there neither is, nor can be any true church in the world, unless it shall be commenced anew by a special commission from heaven. The principle is this; that there can be no valid baptism but upon a credible profession of faith. As it is an acknowledged fact, acknowledged by learned Baptists themselves, that infant baptism was the universal practice of the church for the space of 700 years, that is, from the fourth to the eleventh century, so all their baptisms finally became unlawful or unscriptural, and the church extinct. There is not the remotest probability that there has been a succession of adult baptisms from the days of the apostles. And we conclude those principles which lead to such conclusions as these, can have no foundation in the Scriptures, are unwarranted by Christ, who pledged himself that the gates of hell should never prevail against his church. Such principles, therefore, merely serve the purpose of sectarian distinction. Immersion becomes the shibboleth of a sect; and all that cannot frame their conscience and understanding to pronounce it, are "slain at the fords of Jordan."

Again, the perpetuity of the church and of the covenant made with Abraham, has been conclusively shown, as a fact established clearly by the abundant testimony of the Scriptures. Not only does the Old Testament declare the covenant with Abraham to be everlasting, and including the Gentiles; but the New Testament abundantly shows that the covenant with Abraham could not be abolished by any succeeding dispensations, so that "the promise" should be "of none effect," and that the Gentiles were "grafted into the good olive-tree." The covenant which God made with Israel in the day when he took them by the hand to lead them out of Egypt, could not disannul that covenant, and make the promise of none effect; much less the coming of Christ, and the promulgation of the gospel, and the calling of the Gentiles; for these were the very things which that covenant contained. We have therefore concluded that it is still in force, and its blessings are flowing out to the Gentiles. And also, that it is in force as regards the Jews, and that under it, God will again gather them into his church, grafting them again "into the good olive-tree," and "their children shall be as aforetime," and "so all Israel shall be saved." And as the church had, by the express command of God, been in the habit of applying the seal of the covenant to the children of professed believers, for near 2,000 years, they would, under "the reformation,"or latter dispensation, consider them in the same relation, and apply unto them the "sign of the covenant," and "seal of the righteousness of faith," especially as there is no positive precept forbidding it, and not a word in the New Testament giving the least intimation that such practice was to be discontinued. And as the apostles practised household baptism, and the church uniformly practised infant baptism, therefore we conclude, that it is the will of God and of Jesus Christ, who is "head over all things to the church," that it should be practised still. And there is one case of infant baptism mentioned in the Scriptures, which I would notice in this place. There were a multitude of little ones, or infants, baptized, when all the children of Israel "were baptized unto Moses in the cloud and in the sea,"as they passed through on dry land. When one that rejects infant baptism is referred to this, it is immediately asked, "How do you know that there were any infants there?" A family without infants is possible, but a nation without infants, who ever heard of such a thing? Pharaoh says to Moses, "Go ye serve the Lord,....let your little ones also go with you." "And the children of Israel journeyed from Rameses to Succoth, about six hundred thousand on foot that were men, besides children." All these children, even the little infants, were baptized unto Moses, to be his disciples, and it showed how children could afterwards, together with their parents, be baptized unto Christ, to be his disciples. We therefore have concluded, (and we have no measure of doubt,) that it is agreeable to the will of Christ that children should come unto him in the sacred ordinance of baptism.

If I mistake not, I have attempted to establish nothing upon this subject by assertion. Rather by abundance of proof, both from Scripture and history, has every position been established. And as infant baptism has been practised in every age of the church, from the days of the apostles, so we conclude that it always will be practised, all the prophetic declarations of its opponents to the contrary notwithstanding.

I have no doubt that the positions I have taken will be denied; they have been denied a great many times; but denying a position, does not constitute that position untrue. And asserting a thing to be true, does not make it true.[27] Many attempts have been made, to prove that our positions upon this subject are unscriptural, but no attempt has as yet succeeded; the witnesses always fail to give a plain, unequivocal, direct, and convincing evidence; or even to furnish circumstantial evidence sufficient to establish the incorrectness of our positions. And history absolutely refuses to testify one word against us; when asked to testify against infant baptism, she is perfectly silent, till she comes to the sixteenth century, when she begins to testify through the Anabaptists of Germany. And therefore we conclude that there is no evidence either in the Bible or in history to prove our Paedobaptist views untenable, else the spirit of opposition,and the research of our opponents would have discovered it long since, and have brought it forward with triumphant acclamations. A thousand times it has been boldly asserted that Paedobaptist views were unfounded, and that "there is not a word of Scripture to sustain them," and probably they have wondered that we have not all been convinced by their confident declarations—but still we must be excused for withholding our assent to the truth of declarations, till the evidence in support of them is brought forward. The day has passed away when assertion will pass for proof. Thinking, reflecting minds will demand proof. The best attempts to prove the contrary of our positions have only cast a mist over the subject, and by avoiding the question at issue, and fixing the mind upon something else, numbers have been led into erroneous views upon the subject of baptism.

From two cases of baptism, that of Christ Jesus by John, and that of the eunuch by Philip, it has been concluded by our Baptist brethren, because there is something said about coming "up out of the water" in the one case, and going "down into the water," and coming "up out of the water "in the other, that these baptisms were performed by immersion; when, to warrant them in attaching all the importance they do to the mode, they ought to have, according to their principles, the expressed and unequivocal direction of Christ, so expressed that it would be manifest to every one, that nothing else but that prescribed mode could be baptism. But no such instruction is given, nor any where implied in the Scriptures. Prof. Stuart (who is often quoted by Baptists) has shown conclusively, that the phraseology employed in describing the baptism of Christ and the eunuch, cannot be construed to imply in either case, an immersion. After referring to the baptism of Christ and the eunuch, they next proceed to show that in the early ages of the church, that is, in the third and fourth centuries, baptism was extensively performed by immersion. This is not the point to be proved. We admit that this was the fact.

And we admit that immersion is baptism. The point to be proved to avail them any thing, is not only that immersion was practiced, but that immersion, in the early ages of the church, was considered essential to the validity of baptism. If it is asserted that such was the fact, then we bring the early fathers to testify the contrary, and especially Cyprian, one hundred and fifty years after the apostles, quoting Ezekiel to prove the validity of baptism by sprinkling; and assertions concerning matters of history avail but little against the written testimony of those that lived at the time. And to carry out their principles, they ought to be able to show, that when baptism was administered in any other mode than by immersion, the church refused to permit persons thus baptized, to come to the communion of the Lord's supper; but no attempt is made to show these things.

Again, concerning infant baptism they have never attempted to show that either Christ or his apostles have any where given any precept or instruction whatever, informing the church that children were no longer to be regarded as sustaining a relation to the church; no longer to receive the token of the covenant, and seal of the righteousness of faith. They ought, at least, according to their own principles, to be able to show a positive precept for the abrogation of a principle of the covenant of God, when that principle was established by positive command, for the application of the seal of righteousness to children; for it requires no less authority to abrogate a principle of an institution than to establish it. Whenever the Baptist can bring any positive instructions of Christ, either by himself or apostles, showing that children are no longer to be regarded as sustaining the relation to the church, and holding the place they did in the covenant of God under the Jewish dispensation; how much soever we may regret the being deprived of privileges enjoyed by the church under the former dispensation; how much soever lessened we might suppose our privileges under the gospel dispensation, we should yet feel bound to submit cheerfully, and believe there were reasons for such a course, which we do not now perceive could exist. But no one ever attempts to prove that either Christ or his apostles have given any directions forbidding parents to bring their children to Christ in baptism. Had the apostles so taught, there had been a great murmuring among the Jewish converts.

It is not even supposable that the Jews would without a complaint have given up the relation of children to the covenant, and the sealing of them with the seal of righteousness. And even if that may be supposed, the Scriptures inform us to the contrary. It was years after the introduction of the gospel, and the Jews still supposed that circumcision was to be continued under the gospel dispensation. And it is equally certain that the Jewish Christians under the gospel dispensation understood that their children were still in covenant relation, and that the seal of the righteousness of faith was to be applied to them, as that any of the Jews believed on Jesus Christ. Even the report that Paul taught the Jews that were among the Gentiles, "that they ought not to circumcise their children," created no little commotion among the "many thousands" of Jews at Jerusalem which believed. This was not a question concerning baptism, but circumcision, which the Jews, zealous for the law of Moses, understood was to be practiced under the gospel. And the report created this commotion, because they supposed that laying aside circumcision excluded the children from their connection with the covenant made with Abraham. Then it

is an undeniable fact, that the "many thousands" of Jewish
Christians considered their children as sustaining the same
relation to the covenant of God and to the church, as under
the former dispensation. And when Paul had declared before
the elders that were at Jerusalem, "what things God had
wrought among the Gentiles by his ministry," "they glorified
the Lord, and said unto hirrf, Thou seest, brother, how many
Jews there are which believe, and they are all zealous of the
law; and they are informed of thee, that thou teachest all the
Jews which are among the Gentiles to forsake Moses, saying
that they ought not to circumcise their children, neither to
walk after the customs."

They therefore gave Paul counsel to do those things which
they supposed would do away the impression and allay
the excitement. They say, "As touching the Gentiles which
believe, we have written and concluded that they observe no
such thing, save only that they keep themselves from things
offered to idols, and from blood, and from strangled, and
from fornication."

Now the Baptist says, it is unaccountable, that when the
elders wrote as above to the Gentiles, that they did not say
to them that baptism took the place of circumcision, and
that the baptism of children superseded the necessity of
circumcision. Evidently they said nothing about baptism,
because there was no question about baptism. The question
was concerning certain idolatrous rites, and whether
circumcision and the customs of the Jews should be imposed
upon the Gentile converts. Concerning baptism they were
all agreed; and even those judaizing teachers had made no
complaint that the children of the Gentiles were excluded
from the covenant, Christian baptism being withheld. They
would impose upon both parents and children circumcision

and the law of Moses. So it is manifest that all the Jews, and for several years they constituted the whole Christian church, considered the children as sustaining the same relation to the church, that they had under the former dispensation, and applied to them the token of the covenant, and the seal of the righteousness of faith.

Concerning infant baptism, Baptists themselves must admit, and do admit, that it was generally in use in the Christian church, within a short period of the apostles. But how they account for the fact, that so great an innovation, as they suppose infant baptism to be upon the practice of the apostles, should have been universally adopted by the Christian church without a murmur or a complaint, I know not. That there should not have been one to raise his voice against such an unscriptural practice, as they say it is, seems altogether unaccountable. And if there were any controversy upon the subject, it seems very strange that there should be no record of such controversy, nor allusion to it in any of the writings of the fathers who lived at that time, and whose writings have come down to us. How can it be accounted for, that the most learned men, who lived about three hundred years after the apostles, never heard nor read of any sect or person, not even "the most impious heretic," that denied baptism to infants? And especially, how a great council of sixty-six ministers assembled at Carthage one hundred and fifty years after the apostles, should sit and discuss the point, whether infants might be lawfully baptized before they were eight days old, and none should be found among them to question the propriety of infant baptism, were it then an innovation, but just introduced into the church, I know not. If infant baptism had been introduced into the church at any period between that council and the days of the apostles, they must have known it. And was the church thus early altogether so corrupt that there was not a single minister sufficiently valiant for the truth to lift his voice against this practice, although these were the men that met persecution and death in defence of the gospel of the grace of God: Credat Judaus Apelles, non Ego.

Baptists seldom, if ever, allude to the council of Carthage. And what they do with the whole history of infant baptism, I know not. I recollect having read a history of the Baptist church by a late Baptist writer. There was no difficulty in tracing this church back, by authentic documents, to the sixteenth century; but, beyond that period, there was not a single particle of evidence of the existence of a church in the world upon the principles of the present Baptist denomination, and for this very good reason, that there are no records of the existence of any such church, and that, because no such church had existed; for if there had been any records of such a church they would have been brought forward.

Infant baptism could not have been introduced into the Christian church, at any period subsequent to the days of the apostles, without the fact being on record in the writings of the time, when it was introduced. History points out the time when, and the persons by whom every error was introduced into the church. And it is unaccountably strange, if infant baptism be such a monstrous error as its opponents would have the world think it to be, that this should be the only error introduced into the church, concerning the origin of which no one could give the slightest information; and that this error should have come in, so as to be the universal practice of the church without opposition from any source. Were there any account of the introduction of infant baptism into the church subsequent to the times of the apostles, or even any allusion to such introduction, in the history of the church, would it not be appealed to as indubitable evidence, that it was not the practice of the apostles? Can it be, for a moment, admitted, or even supposed, that so great a change as that of infant baptism would be, on the supposition that the apostles did not practice it, could have been introduced into the Christian church, and there be no scrap of any account of it in the history of the times? That not an individual writer, friend, or enemy, or heretic, should be found to have made the remotest allusion to such fact? It is not supposable. To illustrate the idea; suppose that three-fourths of the whole Baptist denomination should, within the course of the next fifty years, adopt the practice of infant baptism; (and the supposition is not so improbable as the one they make; for they suppose that the whole church from being a Baptist church, as left by the apostles, within a hundred years after the apostles, became Paedobaptist; for it is admitted by the Baptists that in the third and fourth centuries, that is, in the second and third after the apostles, the whole church became Paedobaptist, that is, baptized their infants;) suppose, I say, that such a change should take place in the course of the next fifty years in three-fourths of the Baptist denomination, as they suppose took place during the first century after the apostles, would it not create feeling, remonstrance, and hot discussion? and would not this feeling and discussion be committed to paper, be printed, and handed down in the records of the times to future generations? And could not the time when such defection took place in their ranks, and the place where it commenced, and the persons by whom it was begun, be clearly pointed out two thousand years hence? Most surely.

Upon what subject has the church been divided for these eighteen hundred years that has not been made a matter of controversy? What innovation has been made upon existing practices that has not created opposition, remonstrance, and warm discussion? And that too upon matters of very trivial importance, compared with that of infant baptism. A single individual, Tertullian, who lived within a hundred years of the apostles, advised the delay of infant baptism in certain cases, and the fact is clearly found on the records of history. Had not infant baptism been the practice of the apostles, the moment men began to practice it, that moment a controversy would have commenced concerning it. It would have been disputed at every step of its progress; and could have made but slow advances; and the controversy concerning it would have remained in the history of the times. And its commencement and progress could now be as easily pointed out as we can point out the beginning, progress, and end of the career of Alexander the Great. It can easily be ascertained when men began to oppose infant baptism, and the grounds of their opposition to it. But, if infant baptism was not practiced by the apostles, no one can tell when it began to be practiced. And if it were not a part of the practice and instructions of the apostles, there is an omission in the records of the church that is altogether unaccountable.

On the supposition that the apostles, and all the church after them, practised infant baptism, then the account of the matter in the history of the church, is just what it might have been expected. Then there would of course be no account of the commencement of the practice; but if any should advise to the delay of baptism to children, as did Tertullian; if any should on any account deny infant baptism, as did the

Petrobrusians in the eleventh century, because they thought them incapable of salvation; or if any should deny infant baptism, because they apprehended that faith must precede baptism, as did the Anabaptists in the sixteenth century, then we should expect that such facts would be found in the records of the times when these things took place. And if all the rest of the church had practised infant baptism, we should then find the history of the church expressing the ,fcct as it does. And only on the supposition that all the church practised infant baptism till the times of Augustine and Pelagius in the fourth century, can it be accounted for, that those, the most learned and best-informed men of their day, never heard of any, nay, not even the most impious heretic, that denied infant baptism. It had never been questioned. It had always been considered a practice derived from Christ and the apostles. Therefore we conclude, that infant or household baptism is no innovation upon the practice of the apostolic church, but has uniformly been practiced from the days of the apostles, and was therefore practiced by the apostles themselves; and was, consequently, considered by them as embraced in their commission to disciple and baptize all nations.

Wherefore we conclude, that the denial of infant baptism is an error, an important error;—that it is both anti-scriptural, and anti-historical.

Upon the foregoing view of the subject of baptism, we also conclude, that the practice of close communion is altogether unscriptural, and opposed entirely to the genius and spirit of the gospel which constitutes all Christians one in Christ Jesus. It is founded upon a standard of man's creating; rests upon the opinion of Baptists as to the proper mode of baptism; and was never known in the church till the sixteenth century. It seems to be an assumption of holiness, above their fellow Christians; and says to them, Stand by, for we are holier than you. This is true, if their views are correct. Holiness consists in obedience to the commands of Christ. And here, say they, on the supposition that in all other things we are equal, is one important command which we obey, and you do not; that is, we are immersed and you are not; and they that render the most extensive obedience are the most holy. But then it is an important inquiry, whether, in the views which they adopt concerning immersion, they have not made a commandment for Christ, rather than received his instructions. This being the case, all their conclusions drawn from it, are of course erroneous. Is their assumption, that they are the only true church of Christ, well founded? Have they exclusively the favor of God? Do they appear to be better Christians than others? Are there fewer defections and apostasies among them, than among some other denominations? In what denomination of orthodox Christians has there been so sudden and so extensive a defection as among them, when, within a few years, so large a portion of the denomination has so grossly departed from the truth as to adopt the notion that immersion is regeneration, and that every person assenting to the truth of the Bible is a fit subject for immersion, and that consequently, without immersion there is no regeneration?

An attempt has recently been made in various publications, by the Baptists, to prove to the world that they do not hold to close communion. An attempt to prove that black is white. Close communion is beginning to have an ill savor with an intelligent community; to be abhorrent to Christian feeling, as it is opposed to the spirit of the gospel. The object evidently is, to throw off the odium of close communion. They have really attempted to make the world believe that they do not hold to close communion, after it has been universally admitted and advocated by themselves for these three centuries. They attempt to make men believe that holding to communion with those only who have, according to their views, been properly baptized, and setting aside all those that have been baptized in any other mode, is not close communion! The attempt is unworthy Christian candor, or an ingenuous mind.

How persons can bring themselves to attach such an importance to the mode in which baptism is administered, as to be willing to separate themselves from those whom they acknowledge to be Christians, and whom the Lord blesses with genuine revivals of religion; and especially to separate, themselves from their dearest earthly friends; husbands from their wives; children from their parents, their brothers and sisters, in the communion of the Lord's supper, because they have not been baptized in a particular mode, I am unable to conceive. How it is that they who expect, after a few days, to sit down with their neighbors and friends to the marriage supper of the Lamb, and have the most perfect union and fellowship with them forever in heaven, should be willing to separate entirely from their communion and fellowship here in the kingdom of God on earth, because, in the application of water in the outward ordinance of baptism, it has not been applied to them in the same mode as to themselves, is difficult to conceive. They can receive to their communion those who are full of bitterness, and wrath, and slander; and those who never pray; and those who never speak upon the subject of religion, or scarcely ever, except it be upon the subject of baptism; while others may be most conscientious, pious, godly, and full of the

Holy Ghost; yet if they have been baptized in any other mode than by immersion, their Baptist brethren separate themselves from them as from an "unclean thing."

Is not this close communion contrary to the spirit of all the requirements of the gospel? Are not Christians required to "receive one another as Christ hath received us to the glory of God?" Is it not creating unwarrantable distinctions and division among Christians, when it is the object of the gospel to break down every separating wall, and to constitute all "one in Christ Jesus," to make them "one fold" as they have "one Shepherd?" We cannot believe that it is in accordance with the letter or the spirit of the gospel. Does not the spirit of opposition which it creates and cherishes, gender animosities and strifes; and lead to railing accusations, and a spirit of enmity, which is altogether at variance with the spirit of Christianity? As long as men read the Bible, and imbibe the spirit that is inculcated in its sacred pages, the great body of the disciples of Christ cannot embrace views that lead to such consequences.

"It is a remarkable fact," says Dr. Pond, that missionaries who have left their native country in the belief of the principles of close communion, have not unfrequently renounced them, after laboring for a time among the heathen. This was the case with Mr. Hough, of the American Baptist mission in Burmah. It was the case with the celebrated William Ward, so long a missionary in Bengal. It was the case, too, with the excellent Mr. Chater, of the Baptist mission in Ceylon. Christian missionaries among the heathen are in a favorable situation to feel the influence of Christian love, and the strength of those ties which ought to bind the hearts of Christians together."

Says the person before referred to, formerly a Baptist, in a recent publication:

"Wherefore has the sacred stillness of the Lord's day been interrupted by this repeated travel to the distant stream? Has not the name of God been taken in vain? I searched the Scriptures more carefully and prayed for direction more fervently, and went forward trembling, sustaining close communion another year. I could find no explicit warrant to resist the command of inspiration, 'Receive ye one another as Christ hath received us to the glory of God.' I could find no command for repeating baptism, when it lacked nothing but a little more water. I found, on examination, that no well-read scholar asserted that the Greek word rendered baptism or baptize meant immersion exclusively; and I dared not build exclusive communion on a word which was not itself exclusive. I found my Baptist brethren repeated baptism without explicit warrant; admitted females to the communion without explicit warrant; and without any command, used different elements for symbols of the body and blood of Christ; celebrated the ordinance at a different time, and in a different place from what Christ and his disciples did; and, as I thought, excluded from the table those whom they esteemed Christians, whom they called members of other churches, and all without the evidence of positive precept for making such a use of positive institutions. Having all these things before me, 1 went forward inquiring, and with difficulty continued a Baptist."

Further on he writes,—

"For two years and a half I searched the Scriptures from Genesis to Revelation, with much prayer, that I might know the path of duty. Some of my Baptist brethren spoke lightly of my attention to the Old Testament. I once asked a Baptist brother how he could throw away the precious promises contained in some parts of the 17th chapter of Genesis. He replied, I would not give ninepence for all there is in that chapter. I searched for the command to go down the banks of Jordan, or to be baptized by immersion, and could not find it. I looked for the command to separate children of believers from every token of their parents, and could not find it. When I was baptized, the administrator said, 'Come see the place where the Lord lay.' But when I read the passage, Matthew xxviii. 6, I could not see the justice of its application; and concluded I could not be a Baptist."

Such has been the experience of many of that denomination. Many of them, it is believed, would, even now, break down the wall of separation that divides them from their fellow Christians; they would gladly hold communion with them at the table of Christ; but they cannot without subjecting themselves to discipline, and to excommunication, unless they confess their guilt, and promise to hold to exclusive principles and practice. But the day is approaching, when the wall of separation will be broken down, and the "watchmen shall see eye to eye." There can be no question, but that the great Head of the church will remove every existing evil, and fulfil all his promises to his people; and the church of Christ on earth shall be made to resemble more the church in heaven; when all that love the Lord Jesus Christ shall be of the "same mind" and the "same judgment;" and the whole church shall say, "By one Spirit are we all baptized into one body, whether we be Jews or Gentiles, whether we be bond or free, and have all been made to drink into one Spirit," so shall they have free communion and fellowship one with another. Then so much of the energy of the church will not be wasted in maintaining sectarian interests, and in making proselytes. Then it will be, that love shall reign and triumph, and the glory of the Lord shall be revealed unto all flesh. Be it then our great aim to cherish such a spirit as shall tend to bring about this glorious era in the kingdom of Christ. Let us endeavor to make the terms of Christian communion such, as we may reasonably suppose they will be, in the full millennial glory of the church; such as we know they will be in the kingdom of light and glory, where the saints continually behold the face of their Redeemer. Let us then seek for the "light of the knowledge of the glory of God, as it shines in the face of Jesus Christ," and the influences of "the Spirit of grace and holiness," by which we may be "changed from glory to glory into the same image." And now in view of the whole matter, we conclude that Christ does not regard as essential, rites and forms; and that those Christians who practice sprinkling, and infant baptism, have the approbation of Christ, as they have largely shared in his blessings; and that they will still have his approbation, while they retain the spirit of their Lord and Master. Let us then seek for things which make for peace, and things whereby we may edify one another; extending Christian love, fellowship and communion to all who give evidence that in sincerity and truth they love the Lord Jesus Christ; praying and laboring for the coming and glory of the kingdom of Christ among men.

"The Spirit will at last triumph over the flesh; the love of God, and of fellow Christians redeemed by a Saviour's blood, will burst asunder the manacles of rites and forms, and dispel the charms of sectarian persuasives; and .there will yet be in our American churches, 'one Lord and one faith;' yea, and 'one baptism' also, inasmuch as variety of mode will no longer be regarded as infringing upon the unity of this rite. Yes, those who have been sprinkled by Jesus' blood, and sanctified by his Spirit, will yet be one in him, as he prayed they might be, in his last fervent supplication for them. The Lord hasten these blessed things in their time!" "Even so come Lord Jesus."

ENDNOTES

1. The mere English reader will, perhaps, need to be informed that this is the identical word *baptizo*, in one of its moods and tenses.

2. Mr. Carson, an English Baptist writer, claims that *baptizo* means only to immerse, though he admits that he has all the lexicographers of the Greek language against him. Then it stands Mr. Carson's authority against the authority of all those who for centuries had made the language their study. Who will believe him?

3. Sometime subsequent to the preaching of these discourses, a Baptist clergyman is said to have made certain statements upon this subject, which led the author to address a communication to Prof. Stuart, of which the following is an extract:

"REV. AND DEAR SIR,—

I am credibly informed, that it was stated yesterday, by a Baptist minister, that the most learned Greek scholars in the United States, say that *baptizo* always means to immerse, and nothing else; and especially Prof. Stuart—a man the most learned of any in the languagre—makes the above statement; and also, that at the examination of, the last senior class in the seminary, Prof. Stuart asked one of the students the meaning of *baptizo*, who answered, *to sprinkle*; he asked another, he answered, *to pour*; another, and he answered, *to immerse*: when the Professor instructed them, that the word means always to immerse, and never anything else; and that they must so teach."

To which the Professor returned the following:—

"Andover, Jan. 26, 1836.

MY DEAR, SIR,—

I never said that *baptizo* means only *to immerse*; for it is not true. No such questions were ever asked in the lecture-room, as you mention, at an examination, or at any other time or such answers given by me, or the students, so far as I recollect. The folly of making out such an answer for me, is sufficient]y egregious; inasmuch as my sentiments about the mode of baptism, are before the world—being published some three years since, in a long essay printed in the Biblical Repository, and also in a separate pamphlet, for sale by Gould & Newman, booksellers in this place. "Your friend and obedient servant, "M. STUART."

As Prof. Stuart is continually quoted, or referred to, as sustaining the views of Baptists upon the mode of baptism, I will make a few more extracts from his work—from which, together with those already made, it will be manifest that when his views in full are given, they add but little to the Baptists' arguments in favor of their mode of baptism. Concerning the baptism of Christ, upon which so much stress is laid on account of the expression, 'he went up straightway out of the water,' the Professor remarks, "Both evangelists say that the action of going up took place immediately, or straightway after the baptism. Now if the rite of baptism was completed before John emerged from the water, (in case he was immersed,) i. e. if it was completed merely by the act of plunging him under water, then indeed *anabainon* might possibly be supposed to apply to his emerging from the water. But who will venture to introduce such a conceit as this? Yet if any one should wish to do so, the verb *anabaino* will hardly permit such an interpretation. This verb means, to ascend, mount, go up, viz. a ship, a hill, an eminence, a chariot, a tree, a horse, a rostrum, to go up to the capitol of a country, to heaven, etc. and as applied to trees and vegetables, to spring up, shoot up, grow up. But as to emerging from the water, I can find no such meaning attached to it. The Greeks have a proper word for this, and one continually employed by the ecclesiastical fathers in order to designate emerging from the water; and this is *anaduo*, which means, to *come up out of*—the water,—the ground, etc. But this verb is never commuted, to my knowledge, with *anabaino*. The usage of each seems to be perfectly distinct; yet I do not deny the possibility of employing *anabaino* in the sense of *emerging*. I know the want of accuracy in some writers too well, to hazard the assertion, that no example of such usage can be found. But if there are such examples, they must be very rare. The New Testament surely does not afford them. The preposition apo, (rendered 'out of' in the translation,) will not allow of such a construction. I have found no example, where it is applied to indicate a movement out of a liquid into the air . . . . . *Apo*, denotes either the relation of origin, as sprung from, descended from, etc., or, removal in regard to distance, or the relation of cause to effect, the instrument, etc. To designate emerging from anything that is liquid, I have not found it ever applied.

"These concurrent reasons, both of circumstances and *usus loquendi*, make it a clear case, that Jesus retired from the water of the river, by going up its banks. Nothing more can properly be deduced from it."

Concerning the passage in which it is said, "John also was baptizing in ænon, near to Salim, because there was much water there," after a consideration of the circumstances, the Professor says, "The sacred writer tells us, that 'there went out to him, Jerusalem, and all Judea, and all the neighboring region of Jordan;' and that they were baptized by him. Of course there must have been a great multitude of people. Nothing could be more natural, than for John to choose a place that was watered by many streams, where all could be accommodated. The circumstances of the case, then, would seem to favor that interpretation, which refers the mention of 'many waters,' to the wants of time people who flocked to hear John."

Concerning the baptism of the eunuch, the Professor remarks, that "the real and appropriate signification of this phraseology" (*katebesan amphoteroi eis to udor*, rendered, 'went down both unto the water') "in the New Testament, seems plainly to be, going down to a place. *Katabaino*, designates the action performed in order to arrive there by descending, in any sense; and not the action of entering into the place, to which one has gone down to: although this may sometimes be included, by popular diction. I must come then to the conclusion, that *katebesan amphoteroi eis to udor*, in Acts viii. 38 does neither necessarily nor probably mean, they descended into the water.

This conclusion is rendered nearly certain, by the exact counterpart or antithesis of this expression, which is found in verse 39, where, after the baptism, it is said, *anebesan ex tou udatos*, 'they went up from the water.' We have seen, that *anabaino* is never employed in the sense of emerging from a liquid substance. The preposition *ex*, here, would agree well with this idea, although it by no means of necessity, implies it; but *anabaino* forbids us thus to construe it. As then, to go up from the water, is to ascend the bank of a stream, pool or fountain; so to go down to the water, is to go down the bank of such stream, pool or fountain, and to come to the water. Whether the person thus going down, *eis to udor*, enters into it or not, must be designated in some other way than by this expression, which of itself leaves the matter in uncertainty.

I have another remark to make on *katebesan amphoteroi eis to udor*, they both went down to the water. This is, that if *katebesan eis to udor*, is meant to designate the action of plunging, or being immersed into the water, as a part of *the rite* of baptism, then was Philip as well as the eunuch;—for the sacred writer says that *both* went into the water. Here then, must have been a re-baptism of Philip; and what is at least singular, he must have baptized himself as well as the eunuch.

"All these considerations together, show that the going down to the water, and the going up from the water, constituted no part of the rite of baptism itself; for Philip did the one and the other, just as truly as the eunuch. As then, neither the language allows us to construe the passage as signifying immersion and emersion, nor the circumstances permit us to interpret the passage thus, we have no good and sufficient grounds here to consider this example, as making any determination with respect to the mode of the baptismal rite."

I have extracted thus largely from the Professor's observations upon this case of baptism, as it is the only one in all the Bible, in regard to which there is the remotest allusion made to any kind of motion for the purpose of baptism ; and in this case, he has shown that nothing mole can be implied in the motion specified, than going down from the chariot to the water, and going up the bank from the water to the chariot. And this was just the motion necessary to persons under their circumstances; and the inspired writer, in relating the account, has used the very expressions necessary to describe it intelligibly, on the supposition that Philip baptized the eunuch by sprinkling.

Again he says, "That no injunction is any where given in the New Testament respecting the manner in which this rite shall be performed. If there be such a passage, let it be produced. This cannot be done. But it will doubtless be said, that the 'manner of the rite is involved in the word itself, which is used to designate it; and that therefore, this is as much a matter of command as the rite itself.' To this I answer, that it proves a great deal too much." And he proceeds to show that the Baptist by this would prove himself wrong, while he does not pretend to observe the Lord's supper after the mode in which Christ and his disciples ate it.

Again he says, "Is it essential, in order that baptism should symbolize purification or purity, that it should be performed by immersion? Plainly not; for in ancient times it was the water which was sprinkled upon the offending Jew, that was the grand emblem of purification . . . . . When the whole nation were consecrated to God at Mount Sinai, they, and the book of the law, and the tabernacle, and all the vessels of the ministry, were sprinkled with blood. It is, then, a perfectly clear case, that the sprinkling of water or of blood, was altogether the most significant (ritual mode) of purification, or of atonement, or of consecration to God, under the ancient dispensation.

And so the prophet Ezekiel speaks of water to be sprinkled, under the new dispensation. After describing the gathering in of all the Jews into the kingdom of Christ, he represents Jehovah as saying, 'Then will I sprinkle clean water upon you, and ye shall be clean; from all your filthiness and from all your idols will I cleanse you. A new heart also will I give you.' Is there no significancy, then, in that mode of a rite, which, above all others, is spoken of in the Old Testament and the New, as the emblem of purification and atonement and consecration? Could Jews, who thus spoke and wrote about the application of water and blood by sprinkling, find in sprinkling no due significancy of purification? The question answers itself, after the considerations which have already been suggested. In performing the rite of baptism, then, what are we to aim at?—the shadow or the substance? The substance, enlightened Christians should say. But is not the substance the symbolizing of purity or purification? This, I hope, will not be denied. If, then, water be applied in any such way as to make the symbol or emblem significant or expressive, and highly so, then is the main purpose of the rite answered."

4. William Wall, *The History of Infant Baptism* (LONDON: J. Downing for R. Sympson, 1705)

5. Ibid.

6. Ibid.

7. Ibid.

8. Ibid.

9. Ibid.

10. Orin Fowler, *The Mode and Subjects of Baptism: Four Sabbath evening lectures on the mode and subjects of baptism, preached in November and December, 1834, before the church and congregation to which the author ministers.* (BOSTON: William Peirce, 1835)

11. Ibid.

12. Wall, *The History of Infant Baptism*

13. Enoch Pond, D. D., *A treatise on the Mode and Subjects of Christian Baptism: in Two Parts—Designed as a reply to the statements and reasonings of the Rev. Adoniram Judson, Jun., as exhibited in his "Sermon, preached in the Lal Bazar chapel, Calcutta, on Lord's-Day, September 27, 1812.* (WORCHESTER: William Manning, 1818)

14. In the *Encyclopedia of Religious Knowledge*, is the following statement in the article entitled Mennonites: "We have now seen that the Baptists, who were formerly called Anabaptists, and in later times Mennonites, were the original Waldenses and who have long in the history of the church received the honor of that origin. On this account the Baptists may be considered as the only Christian community which has stood since the days of the apostles, and as a Christian society which has preserved pure the doctrines of the gospel through all ages." This is taking most tremendous strides. With one foot upon a baseless fabric in the 16th century, with the other, at a single step, he strides quite up to the days of the apostles, nor touches ought in the whole distance. First it is assumed that the Mennonites were the original Waldenses, without any foundation, and that therefore the Baptist denomination has stood ever since the days of the apostles. A truly convenient method of proving

the antiquity of the Baptist denomination. That the above statement is without foundation may be seen by referring to the article, from which the above is extracted and the article entitled Menno, in the same work. It will there be seen that Menno was born in 1505, and that it was not till 1530, that he seriously examined the New Testament, though a "Romish priest," and that after this period, he united himself with the Anabaptists and became a preacher of that order in 1537, about twenty years after the commencement of the reformation under Luther. It is not even claimed for him that he had any relation to the Waldenses. It is a well known fact that the Anabaptists were in the city of Munster about 1521. They were not Waldenses, nor of them, but a class of fanatical reformers, whose fanatical proceedings required a military force to keep the peace. That some of those who were the descendants of the Waldenses, who were driven from their country by persecution into Bohemia and neighboring countries, may have, about the time of Menno, united with the Anabaptists, is possible. But how this should have constituted the Anabaptists the original Waldenses is rather difficult to conceive. The attempt to confound the Mennonites with the Waldenses has its origin, probably, from the desire of finding some other ancestry for the Baptist denomination than the Anabaptists of Munster. In the article referred to, it is said,— "There were two sects among them: the one distinguished by the name of the *perfect* (who held to a community of goods) and the other the *imperfect*. By far the greater part of the first sect, and the whole of the second, were certainly among the most pious Christians the church ever saw, and the worthiest citizens the state ever had." This is so connected with some reference to the Waldenses in their scattered state, as to lead the reader to suppose that this account of the "two sects," was an account of the Waldenses when by referring to the article Anabaptists in the same work, it will be perceived to be an account of them, and not of the Waldenses. Then follows a section, stating that Menno gathered these "two sects" into "a regular church state," still carrying the idea, that it was the Waldenses thus gathered into "a regular church state," when it was the Mennonites. Then follow the remarks quoted at the beginning of this note, and the conclusion there drawn, that the Anabaptists or Mennonites, otherwise called Baptists, were the original Waldenses a conclusion altogether unwarranted—at least the article itself does not furnish the data for any such conclusion. Nor does it furnish any evidence that the Anabaptists or Mennonites had any connection with, or relation to, the Waldenses, much less that they were the "original Waldenses." Wherefore the conclusion, that the Waldenses were Baptists is unfounded. And even if it were true that the Waldenses were Baptists (which they were not), how does it thence follow that the Baptist denomination has stood ever since the days of the apostles? There was a long period between the apostles and the Waldenses, and the writers of that period say nothing about a Baptist church, but much to the contrary.

15. When men are determined upon sustaining a particular doctrine, the flat contradiction of that doctrine by an inspired apostle is a matter of very little weight in their estimation. I recollect once hearing a Friend Quaker preach, (this denomination of Quakers reject all water baptism,) and when Peter withstood him to the face, saying, in the case of Cornelius and his friends, "Who can deny water that these should not be baptized?" he thrice excused the weakness

of Peter in baptizing them with water, then proceeded in his discourse.

16. Wall, *The History of Infant Baptism*, Part 1, chap. 2, page 23.

17. In an article on baptism by Prof. Knowles in the Encyclopedia of Religious Knowledge, are the following among other unfounded assertions and statements, that:

> "In every case of baptism recorded in the Scriptures, some facts are stated which assert or imply that the persons baptized were believers. There is on the other hand, not a single example in the New Testament of the baptism of an infant, nor one word which fairly implies it. It is expressly said of the Philippian jailer and his household, that they all believed, and though the same assertion is not made respecting the households of Lydia and Stephanas, yet other circumstances are stated, which imply that none of the members of those families were infants."

These are broad and sweeping assertions—and most unfounded assertions, having nothing but the ipse dizit of him that makes them, to rest upon. The opposite of these assertions has been a thousand times proved. I know not how to account for it, that a man like Prof. Knowles should make these unqualified statements, unless it be on the strength of party feeling. I ask, what fact is stated in the Bible, or even alluded to, which implies that Lydia's household were believers? What circumstances are stated which imply that there were no infants in her household? I reply, without the fear of any proof to the contrary ever being brought, none—absolutely none whatsoever, unless found in these assumed positions of the Baptists, that none but adult believers are proper subjects of baptism, and then as these were baptized, it follows that they were both adults and believers. In regard to the assertion, that there is not in the New Testament, a single example of the "baptism of an infant, nor one word which fairly implies it," I have only to say, that it savors strongly of that spirit, which, when facts and arguments are wanting, is determined to carry its point by bold and brow-beating assertions, made in the face of the learning and wisdom of nine-tenths of the Christian church, for these seventeen centuries. It boldly affirms, that the opinion or judgment of the great body of learned men, who have examined the subject, is without foundation. There is not a little of arrogance in it. In regard to the assertion, that "it is expressly said of the Philippian jailer and his household, that they all believed," I hardly know how to reconcile this with knowledge and Christian candor, unless the Professor means, that it is expressly so stated by the Baptists; for I affirm, as I have shown, that it is not so said in the Bible; nor is there anything in the Bible that implies it, unless it be in what a Baptist would consider sufficient proof, the fact that they were baptized. Luke says not one word about the family of the jailer having believed, as anyone may see by turning to Acts xvi. 34, in the Greek Testament. And how the Professor, with the Greek Testament in his hand, could make such assertion, I know not.

18. Wall, *The History of Infant Baptism,* Part 1, pg. 23.

19. Ibid., Part 1, pg. 25.

20. Ibid., Part 2, pg. 452.

21. Ibid., Part 1, pg. 54.

22. Ibid., Part 1, pg. 78,79.

23. Ibid., Part 1, pg. 426.

24. Ibid., Part 1, pg. 432.

25. John L. von Mosheim, *Institutes of Ecclesiastical History: Ancient and modern, in four books, much corrected, enlarged, and improved from the primary authorities, John Lawrence von Mosheim; a new and literal translation, from the original Latin, with copious additional notes, original and selected, in three volumes,* James Murdock, ed./trans. (NEW YORK: Harper, 1839.) 2nd ed., rev. and enl., Volume III, pg. 473.

26. Orin Fowler, *The Mode and Subjects of Baptism: Four Sabbath evening lectures on the mode and subjects of baptism, preached in November and December, 1834, before the church and congregation to which the author ministers.* (BOSTON: William Peirce, 1835)

27. The community will, in time, learn that bold declarations are not proof. And slanderous stories about Congregational deacons; and what "they say" that certain Paedobaptist ministers have told individuals, etc. etc. are neither argument nor proof against our positions.

For another classic on baptism read—

A Great Christian Book

Immersion
It Is Not Baptism

John H. Beckwith

Available at
www.greatchristianbooks.com

For a catalog of other great Christian books including additional titles on Baptism—

contact us in any of the following ways:

write us at:
Great Christian Books
160 37th Street
Lindenhurst, NY 11757

call us at:
(631) 956-0998

find us online:
www.greatchristianbooks.com

email us at:
mail@greatchristianbooks.com

www.ingramcontent.com/pod-product-compliance
Lightning Source LLC
Chambersburg PA
CBHW020155090426
42734CB00008B/834